DUCHESSE LACE

Fig. 1. *'The Lace-maker' by
Caspar Netscher, 1664*
*Reproduced by permission of
the Trustees, the Wallace
Collection, London*

DUCHESSE LACE

Jane Newble-de Graaf

'. . . One can understand that to
connoisseurs and lovers of valuable lace,
Duchesse is very dearly prized.'

Louisa Tebbs[1]

B. T. Batsford Ltd · London

For Nicholas and Rhoda Jane

First published 1989

0 7134 5629 9

*Typeset by Deltatype Ltd, Ellesmere Port
and printed in Great Britain by The Bath Press, Bath
for the publishers
B. T. Batsford Ltd
4 Fitzhardinge Street
London w1h 0ah*

Contents

Acknowledgements

There are many people who have, directly and indirectly, helped in the writing of this book, although it is impossible to mention them all.

I am most grateful to Jean Chesters, without whom I might never have made lace, and to Theodora Smolders-Walgraeve, who stimulated my early interest in lace.

I should like to thank my students in Mold, Clwyd, for their enthusiasm, and my British friends, who have encouraged me by their interest and advice, in particular Marcus and Olive Crouch, and Geoffrey Crine.

Without my Dutch friends the book would have been much more difficult to complete. I am thinking especially of Marijke van Wijngen and Nora Ummels who lent me some of their designs, and of Dine v.d. Rijst-Middelkoop.

Thanks also go to the staff in the museums in Holland and England, for all their assistance.

I am grateful to my parents, Mr and Mrs L. J. de Graaf-Lammerink, of Ommen, and to my sister, Henny de Graaf, for their help on the 'Dutch side', in making all practical problems so very much easier, and to my father-in-law, Mr E. F. Newble, of Deal, for making my unique and much-used workbox.

In addition, I should like to express my gratitude to John May, President of the Winchester Photographic Society, who came to our rescue in printing the photographs, and to Ann Collier, for her willingness to write a foreword according to Dutch tradition.

Credit also goes to the Publishers of the works used for relevant quotations to introduce the chapters.

Special thanks go to my husband Alan L. Newble, for his labour in taking all the photographs, for his valuable advice, and for providing me with much-needed days of solitude.

I want to thank my children for their ability to make themselves unheard and unseen on so many occasions, and for cheerfully putting up with fewer home-made cakes than usual.

Finally, I should like to thank the people of Alresford for welcoming us the way they did, and for making living here such a pleasure.

Alresford, 1989
Jane Newble-de Graaf

8

Foreword

One of the most popular laces of the 19th century and consequently one of those still to be found in antique markets is Duchesse. The scrolling leaves and flowers made it a great favourite of the Victorian ladies who wore it as dress flounces, shawls, collars and fans. It was often combined with needle lace and the two techniques complement one another very well.

It is often mistaken for Honiton as the techniques are very similar, but in Duchesse we find the primrose and a few fillings and in Honiton there is the rose and many more fillings. The lace-makers of today are finding that the more techniques that they can master, the better is their lace – bobbin-lace-making seems to have no end to its learning.

The techniques of Duchesse are so well illustrated in this book that a novice can learn it, or practised lace makers can perfect another skill, and because it is so adaptable and requires no pricking, it opens up a whole new world of design to the ambitious.

I am so pleased that after so many years we now have an English textbook about this delightful lace.

Ann Collier

Introduction

'The letters or the words of a book are nothing, but the thought they give is real.'

Richard Jefferies[2]

As you are reading this book, you presumably love lace, lace-making, or fine art in general. For me, lace-making is not just a skill, but also a form of art. Lace-work can be dead and sterile, or it can be alive with beauty and individuality. On my way through museums I have seen lifeless, uninspired pieces of lace, mere shapes of woven thread, although skilfully made. At the same time, I have seen lace which fired my imagination, and affected me in the way

Fig. 2. *Dutch headdress, worn in Ommen, trimmed with 'Rijssels' lace (property of Mrs Vosjan)*

paintings, poetry or music do. In particular I am thinking of the work of Elena Holeczyova, which has fascinated me by its charm and originality ever since I first saw it. Lace with this impact is my ideal of what lace should be. Perhaps that is why I have a special love for Duchesse, mainly the type of Duchesse developed in Holland, my native country.

During childhood I came into contact with lace on my grandfather's farm. My grandmother wore the traditional regional Dutch costume, on which the head-dress was trimmed with 'Rijssels' lace (fig. 2). The head-dress was called 'cornetmuts', and was later known as 'knipmuts' or 'neepjesmuts'. It may be interesting to mention that this head-dress was first worn in Paris, before 1800, and from there became widely used in many areas in Holland, with regional differences.[3] It was made of fine white cotton, gathered

Fig. 3. *The author's sister, wearing the Dutch costume*

into tiny folds at the top, with lace covering the head, and falling down to the shoulders (fig. 3). Only very few women now wear this costume, but happily, I inherited a costume with head-dress from a great-aunt.

Even after my grandmother died, I remained interested in intricate types of lace, and became even more so after becoming friends with the daughter of a Belgian lace-maker, who gave me several pieces of lace made by her mother.

Yet it was not until years later that I met Jean Chesters, who shares my love of art and lace. We did not need much encouragement, and taught ourselves the art in her home in North Wales, even making our own bobbins.

Apart from the actual contact with lace, I have always been attracted by the beauty in the shape and form of flowers. To try and express some of the beauty of nature in a stylized way in Duchesse gives me great joy and satisfaction.

Before getting into Duchesse lace, it may be helpful to some of you if I briefly explain the main difference between the well-known types of lace. There are basically two types of bobbin-lace, known as continuous and non-continuous lace.

In *continuous* lace, the number of bobbins remains the same throughout the work. Some examples of this type of lace are Torchon, Valenciennes, Binche, Flanders and Bucks Point (fig. 4).

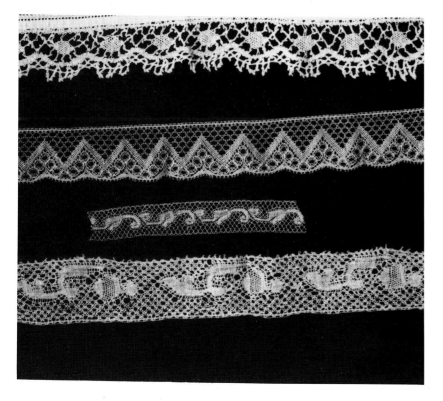

Fig. 4. *Examples of some continuous types of lace (from top to bottom): Bedfordshire, Bucks Point, Valenciennes, Flanders*

Fig. 5. *Examples of non-continuous types of lace (top right to bottom left): Bruges flower-lace, Honiton, Brussels Duchesse, Early Flanders, probably 17th century*

In *non-continuous* bobbin-lace, motifs are worked with a varying number of bobbins, and are connected by bars, sewings and fillings. Examples of this type of lace are Honiton, Bruges flowerwork and Duchesse (fig. 5).

This book obviously concentrates on Duchesse lace, but the purpose of it is to help you make this lace in your own way, and to encourage you to design your own patterns. Should you already make Duchesse lace, it may inspire some new ideas. Often there is more than one way of doing the same thing, so if you find a better, quicker or easier way – wonderful! I'd love to hear about it, too. By the way, do get into the habit of making notes while you are experimenting. It does help if you can verify afterwards what it was that you did differently.

Although it is not necessary to be an experienced lace-maker, in using this book it will be helpful if you can work the basic general lace-techniques. Most of all, this book is meant to give you a working knowledge of the Duchesse techniques, and to create a desire to improve and invent.

When, as happens to most of us, you feel bogged down by

repeated failure of a certain technique, my advice is – make yourself a cup of tea, and try something else. It is amazing how seeing things from a different angle clears your mind, and gives you a fresh insight into something. You will then have the courage to come back to it and try again. Anyway, a first imperfect flower is just the thing to sew on to a tiny cushion for a little girl's doll's house. I know someone who walked off highly delighted with one-third of a cloverleaf that I had just abandoned. She had never seen Duchesse lace, had no hope of ever trying to make it, and thought it was exquisite. So you see, what you do not like may appeal to someone else.

In the first chapters, where you may still be working your way through the exercise pieces, I have given the number of bobbins to use, and the type of thread, so that you will gain confidence more quickly. As you become more experienced, you will be able to work out how many bobbins you need for certain patterns.

Not many technical diagrams are included, because not everyone gets on with them, and especially for beginners they can be rather confusing. They are invaluable for a continuous lace-type, like Flanders or Valenciennes, but for Duchesse they can seem too complicated, unless you are used to them. Consequently, I have tried to keep my diagrams simple, and have divided them into stages of working, where possible. I hope you find them useful that way. In most diagrams I have used a single line for one pair of bobbins, but where I thought it would be particularly useful, I have given the line-drawings.

After the last chapter you will find an example of the method I use to make a design, in a step-by-step explanation.

To conclude – practice is all important, not only for accuracy, but especially if you want to develop a personal and beautiful style of lace-making. Do not expect too much of yourself too soon. The hours spent in working a dozen flowers or cloverleaves will repay you, in time, as well as confidence.

Fig. 6. *Handkerchief corner, from the work of Mien Nulle (1904–06)*
Reproduced by permission of Boymans-van Beuningen Museum, Rotterdam

1 History of Duchesse

'I caught myself thinking of little insects incessantly spinning these things, and who, on that account, are left in peace. No, of course, they were women! "They have surely gone to heaven, those who made it," I said admiringly.'

R. M. Rilke[4]

Duchesse lace is in origin a Belgian lace, named after Marie Henriette, duchess of Brabant, who married the future king Leopold II of Belgium in 1853. It was made during and since the second half of the 19th century, and it was often combined with motifs worked in needle-lace. Because of its intricate design, it was

Fig. 7. *Map of Holland with relevant towns*

• Ommen

Amsterdam •

• Apeldoorn

. The Hague

Rotterdam .

• Sluis

17

highly prized, and became more and more known. In a report of the Jury of the Paris exhibition of 1855, an Aerschot firm was awarded a medal for lace called 'duchesses'.

About the same time, in 1854, a lace-school was established in Sluis, in the south-west of Holland (fig. 7). After five years the school won a silver medal, and the list of items makes it clear that a lot of Duchesse lace was made and exhibited. During the heyday of this school it was said that more than 130 girls and women were working there.[5] Because of the slump in the lace-industry, and the outbreak of the Franco-Prussian war in 1870, the school was closed in 1872.

In 1884 a girl was born, called Mien Nulle. She would have a very significant influence on the development of lace in the Netherlands, and would be recognized as one of the greatest experts in lace. From her youth she loved needlework, and knew exactly what she liked and wanted to do. Unfortunately, when she went to the Technical School in The Hague, the needlework-classes there were not at all to her liking. She insisted on doing what she wanted to do – fine work, instead of the course work that was taught. She upset everyone by this attitude, including her parents, but she persevered and taught herself to make bobbin-lace. At the same time she took lessons on Saturday afternoons from a servant, who was a former pupil of the Sluis lace school. Together with her study at the Technical School, where she was also taught drawing and art history, this made her very knowledgeable on the subject of lace. So much so, that at the final exam in 1903, she received the Heemskerck Prize for the best pupil in the school. It was an inscribed gold thimble, which is now kept in the Rijksmuseum in Amsterdam. During these years, handmade lace was still very much in demand.

It did not take long before her work was 'discovered' by someone important, and in 1903 she became a teacher at the new lace school in Apeldoorn. This school had been opened in 1902 with Agathe Wegerif-Gravestein as director. The emphasis in the school was on making fine lace, learning to draw, and developing the artistic ability to design (fig. 8).

It is interesting that there was severe opposition to the opening of this school. Some said that lace-making was bad for the eyes, and damaging to health, referring to a lot of illness among Belgian lace-makers. Others said that it was quite unnecessary to make 'real' lace, because there was such beautiful machine-made imitation lace available.

The author of an article in the then popular women's magazine *Eigen Haard* complained in 1902 that the opposition was a result of jealousy in the minds of those who find it difficult to give others the credit for doing something well. He advised: 'The most sensible thing to do is not to trouble oneself about the shouting of these

land waar
; meer dan
eeuwen het
werken een
ofdindustrie
en nog steeds
ls een ideale
t gewenschte
tand wordt be-
ruwd, blijkens
n schrijver.
ook de onder-
ning van den
it wenscht in
vorm van het
en van subsi-
1, het inrichten
localiteiten,

schat wordt,
geboren uit
duldige to
dingsliefde.
geen honge
nen, geen v
oude, voor
tijd versleten
vinnen van
arbeid, maar
zonde, nij
werksters, di
de zenuw
kende lucht
Veluwe de vr
ten genieten b
kunstvaardigl
Als een b

Gedeelte van een platte kraag, point Duchesse, naar moderne teekening.
Vervaardigd aan de kantwerkschool te Apeldoorn.

, — dit alles vinden wij in onze Nederlandsche kant-
kschool. Hier wordt aan haar, die vroeger genood-

van de gunstige gevolgen voor een geheele streek, w
de oprichting eener kantwerkschool hebben kan, citee

Gedeelte van een afhangende kanten kraag, point Duchesse, moderne teekening. Vervaardigd aan de Nederlandsche Kantwerkschool te Apeldoorn.

aakt waren als naaister, dienstbode, enz, in haar onder-
oud te voorzien, de gelegenheid geboden zich te bekwamen
n een vak, dat verheft, dat, vol poëzie, de oogen opent voor
ie schoonheid van het teedere en fijne, hetwelk zij kunnen
eggen in het werk harer handen, dat haar een kostbare

hier nog even wat de heer Pierre Verhaegen in
ganoemd boekje over de school van Burano zegt:
„Les conditions de la vie sont devenues satisfaisai
à Burano, et dans les îles environnantes on trava
activement aux fuseaux. A Burano, les jeunes dentelli
sont particulièrement recherchées et mariage par les jeu

Fig. 8. *Page of magazine,*
Eigen Haard, from 1902

people, and to proceed in the course once taken.' He also reported that lace-making is not damaging to eyes or health, and that the bad health of many lace-makers in Belgium was due to being taken advantage of by unscrupulous traders.[6]

Any girl who wanted to be admitted to the school had to be 12 years of age, and the course lasted one year.

After having taught at the school for a year, in 1905, Mien Nulle became the new director. She very much encouraged the girls to design lace-patterns, by teaching them step-by-step to stylize flowers and other shapes in nature. A lot of Duchesse was made at the school, which was mainly used then for wedding-handkerchiefs and fine collars.

Under her guidance the school flourished, and in 1906 it was moved to The Hague, closer to the buying public, as the quality of the lace was excellent, and the interest in hand-made lace was growing. Even when she married in 1907 and became Mrs v.d. Meulen-Nulle (in Holland girls keep their maiden-name when they marry), she left her husband in Apeldoorn four days each week in order to keep the school in The Hague going. Obviously, her husband must have been ultra-modern and very proud of her work, not to stand in the way, or make things difficult for her. At this time she also wrote the handbook on Duchesse which was re-written in 1983 by the Dutch lace-teacher and lecturer Zus (Dorothea) Boelaars.[7]

In 1911 Mrs v.d. Meulen-Nulle left the school, which was closed in 1918 as a result of the First World War. She felt that she wanted to be more active in other ways, and for the next four years she gave courses throughout the country, and many private lessons. In 1915 she and her husband went to the Dutch East Indies and returned in 1919, after also having been in San Francisco and New York. From the date of her return, she travelled all over the country by train to teach lace, and to carry on the lace tradition.[8]

The Dutch Queen Emma, who herself always wore lace, and had already shown much interest in the lace school in The Hague, also appointed Mrs v.d. Meulen to look after the royal lace (fig. 9). One of the characteristics of her work and teaching was her accuracy in style and drawing, which resulted in lace of superior quality. Dutch lace was much in demand at that time, especially by visitors from America. In 1920 she was asked to wash all the lace in the Rijksmuseum and prepare it for display. She also helped to establish a lace society in Holland, 'Het Kantsalet', which was founded in 1925.

Just before the Second World War, by 1935 all the lace schools had closed – even the one in Sluis, which had re-opened in 1910, during the days when lace-making flourished again. There was much less demand for lace now, and wearing hand-made lace was a

Fig. 9. *Dutch stamp of 1934, picturing Dowager Queen Emma*

great luxury. However, Mrs v.d. Meulen kept working, and published another book on lace.[9] She had a great influence in the revival of interest in lace in the Netherlands, and in 1979, when she was 95, she was decorated with the Order of Oranje-Nassau, a tremendous honour.

For a long time lace had been made by a few dedicated women, but the renewed interest meant that there was a sudden demand for Mrs v.d. Meulen's book on Duchesse. It was rapidly sold out, and not until it was re-written in 1983 was there a book available on this lace-technique. Mrs v.d. Meulen was a personality, and people who met her were impressed by her dignity and charm, and her deep love for lace.

There was a further development of Duchesse lace in a convent called Klooster Withof, in the south of Holland. One of the nuns, Sister Judith, who had been at the Sluis school, is now teaching this beautiful technique under the name of 'Withof Duchesse'.

Duchesse has again become a well-known and much-loved type of lace, offering opportunities for interesting designs, both symmetrical and free in form and style. For anyone interested in 'free lace' the techniques of Duchesse are indispensable.

2 Equipment for making Duchesse lace

'Yon cottager, who weaves at her own door,
Pillow and bobbins all her little store;

William Cowper, *'Truth'*[10]

It is a little store indeed, which is used for the actual making of lace. However, you will need a few more tools than just those that are obvious to onlookers.

Fig. 10. *Page from* Table Talk, *by William Cowper, published in 1825*

23

The list varies according to the type of lace. For Duchesse you will need the following:

Pillow and covercloths
Bobbins and bobbin-box or -case
Pins, pincushion and pin-lifter
Duchesse hook for sewings
Thread
Patterns
Accessories for travelling

Pillow and covercloths

A Duchesse pillow is large, round and flat, sloping down from the middle, with a diameter of 50 or 60cm (20 or 24in) (fig. 11).

Cover the pillow with a piece of cotton or linen, which can be washed. On the Continent very often a printed material is used, but dark blue or green is more restful for your eyes.

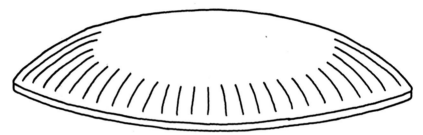

Fig. 11. *Dutch lace pillow*

You also need a cloth with a round hole in the middle, so that you can work a small area of lace, unhindered by pins already in the work (fig. 12). This cloth is called 'gatlap' in Dutch. The hole is

Fig. 12. *Measurement of the hole in the cover cloth*

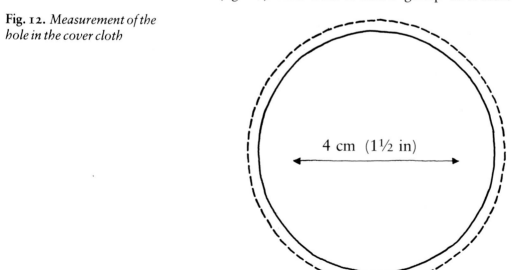

4 cm (1½ in)

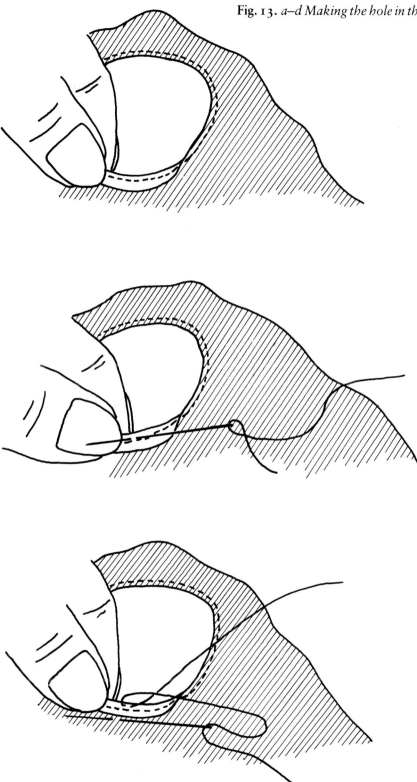

Fig. 13. *a–d Making the hole in the cover cloth with a rolled hem.*

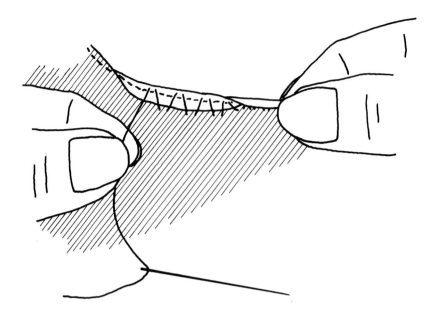

finished with a rolled hem, and has a diameter of 4cm (1½in). For making the rolled hem see figs. 13a–d. You need one more cloth to cover the lace when you are not working on it. This will keep the lace clean and free from dust. Of course this can be any decorative piece of material. I use a large Dutch handkerchief and put it on my knees while I am working, so that I am more likely to remember to put it on the pillow whenever I leave the work.

Fig. 14. *Pillow in use*

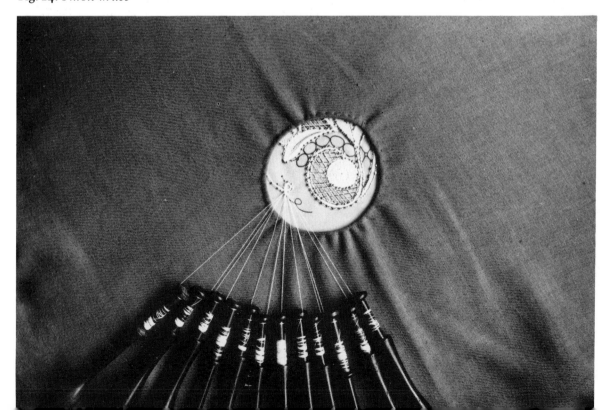

Bobbins and bobbin-box or -case

In his famous dictionary Samuel Johnson describes the bobbin as: 'A small pin of wood, with a notch, to wind the threads about when women weave lace.' Many different types of bobbins are used, according to the type of lace and the country or area in which it is made. For Duchesse lace, a small Flemish bobbin is used (fig. 15).

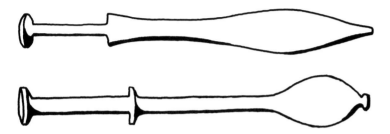

Fig. 15. *Two Duchesse bobbins*

The pointed end makes sewings easier, like the bobbins used in Honiton lace. The total number of bobbins you need is hardly ever more than 18 pairs. An advantage with this lace is that you can rewind those bobbins that have been laid out of the work, and use them again in the same pattern. Duchesse bobbins are mostly made of palmwood or rosewood. I like to keep my bobbins together with other tools in a bobbin-box, which can be anything from a wooden purpose-built box to a large decorative biscuit-tin.

Fig. 16. *Small selection of bobbins from different countries: Scandinavian, Czechoslovakian, Dutch, British, French, Belgian*

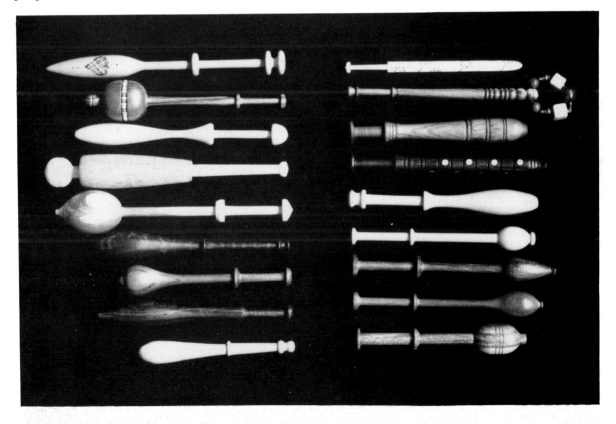

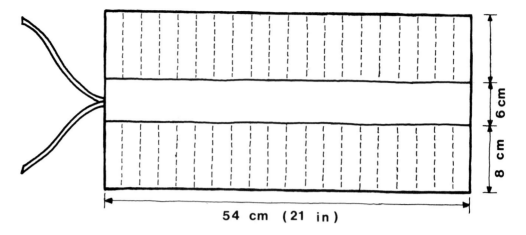

Fig. 17. *Working drawing of a bobbin-case*

When you have pairs of already-wound bobbins, you will find it useful to store them in a bobbin-case. This is very easy to make from a left-over piece of material, and can be rolled up and tied. For measurements, see fig. 17.

For immediate use it is handy to hang wound pairs on a bobbin-tree. This is of similar design to a 'mug-tree', but the arms stick out horizontally, and have grooves in them.

Fig. 18. *Bobbin tree in use*

Pins and pin-lifter

In Duchesse lace the very fine short pins are used (17mm, ⅝in), as you often need to press them right down into the pillow. They are made of brass, so that there will be no rust marks on the lace, when you leave the work for a long time. A small pincushion is the best way to store and use pins. The one I use is stuffed with emery powder mixed with lavender. It removes the tarnish from the pins, and at the same time smells sweetly when used, if you like lavender.

Longer pins like hat pins are useful for securing the pincushion to the pillow, fastening the bobbins when travelling, and shortening threads.

The pin-lifter is a most useful instrument, and essential for preserving your nails! It has a flat end for pressing the pins right down, and a 'fork' for pulling them out (fig. 19).

Fig. 19. *Some tools for Duchesse lace: pins, Duchesse hook and pin-lifter*

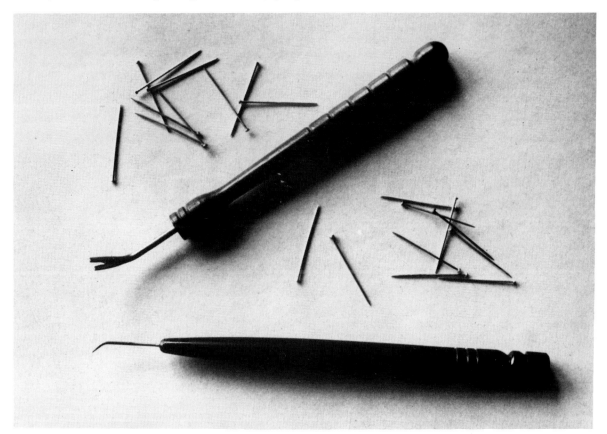

Duchesse hook for sewings

The Duchesse hook is slightly different from the needle-pin. The needle is curved at the end, so that it looks like a hook. It is a joy to use, as it is a little more manageable than a straight needle. Some people like to use a wig-hook, but with this you have to be careful not to catch the fine thread and break it. You can of course use the Honiton needle-pin if you are more used to that.

Thread

Traditionally Duchesse was made with fine cotton, up to No. 500. It used to be sold in skeins, tied together with red-coloured thread. This is not now available, and the finest is No. 180. The thickness varies with the pattern, and personal preference. Most Duchesse patterns range from No. 80 to No. 140. In this book Belgian Brok and Egyptian cotton have been used.

Fig. 20. *Old thread, thought to be No. 250, and Egyptian and Brok cotton, No. 100*

When working large patterns, or several patterns in the same thickness of thread, you could find it helpful to wind rather a lot of thread on one bobbin, the 'mother-bobbin', and then wind short lengths on the 'partner-bobbin' as you need it.

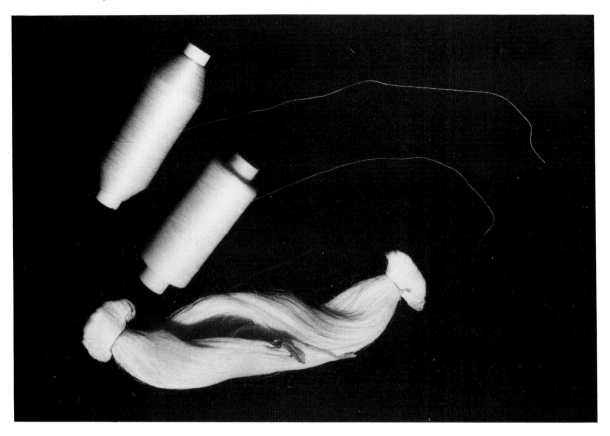

Patterns

In Dutch a pattern is often called a 'kantbrief', literally translated as 'lace-letter'. It really means that you can read a pattern like you read a letter, and interpret it your way. Someone else reading the same letter would notice different things in it. There is no need to follow the pattern slavishly. You can put your own ideas into it, providing you know the techniques, and the finished lace has been carefully thought out and worked.

In Duchesse lace there is no pricking. The pattern is an outline drawing, with a clear indication of the stitches and fillings used (fig. 21). You determine the distance between the pins as you are working, which gives a certain amount of freedom and individuality. However, practice is necessary!

Fig. 21. *'Rachel', an example of a Duchesse pattern-drawing.*

Traditionally, a thin green card is used for the pattern, so that pins can be set without much difficulty. The pattern is drawn with waterproof ink, never with ball-point or pencil, as these could discolour the thread.

However, there are other ways of preparing a pattern. You can photocopy the pattern and cover it with a matt, coloured, sticky transparent film; or trace the pattern on tracing-paper, and cover this with the film; you put this combination on the pillow, with a piece of white paper underneath it.

Another method is to use carbon paper (very lightly) and draw over this with waterproof ink. Alternatively, you can use tracing paper, trace the pattern with waterproof ink, pin this on a piece of thin card, and start working. Pin the pattern on to the pillow with a pin in each corner, pressed down very firmly. Then put the cloth with the hole over the pattern, leaving visible the place where you start working.

Accessories for travelling

From time to time you will want to take your pillow with you when travelling. The easiest and safest way of securing the bobbins to the pillow is to crochet a long strip with small holes next to each other. This prevents the threads breaking. Put each bobbin-head into a hole, and pin this strip down on the pillow at each end. This will also keep them in place, and you will waste no time untangling bobbins.

Over the whole pillow you pin your covercloth, and put the pillow in a large pillow-bag. Very strong imitation-leather ones are available on the Continent, or you might be able to make one from very strong cotton or linen.

3 Basic techniques

'I think my fingers must be all thumbs.'
A. T. Quiller-Couch[11]

When you first try out a completely different kind of lace, you often feel a mixture of excitement and apprehension. The apprehension gradually disappears through practice, and will give way to a feeling of confidence as you begin to master the new techniques. The excitement, however, grows with each new pattern you try out. It is important to take great care at the beginning: practise too much rather than not enough. It is worth it!

When you can work the first pieces easily, without having to refer to written instructions every few minutes, then you can proceed to the next one.

There is, probably for most of us, a temptation to jump ahead, and we can end up not really knowing the basic rules. Being methodical, and working through the patterns step-by-step, repays in the end. I would advise you to practise the individual items like flowers and leaves until you can sit somewhere, anywhere, without a book, and make one. With half-a-dozen flowers you can make a lovely appliqué round the neck of a dress, or work them round a little mat. There are basic techniques in Duchesse which you will have to use in almost every pattern, and it is vitally important to really get to know these, so that you can do them without referring to a book.

The big advantage of Duchesse is that there is no pricking. What a time-saver! However, that does mean that it is important to practise spacing the pins, so that the result looks neat and tidy, and the weaver threads are at right-angles to the footside (fig. 23). I have given some practice braids here: these are worked without a gimp thread, and with different thicknesses of thread (fig. 24).

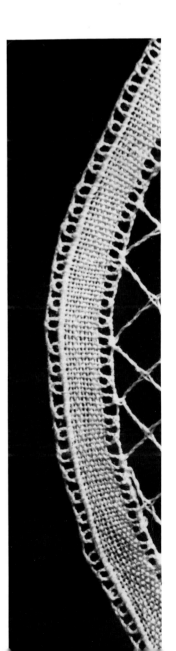

Fig. 22. *The angle of weaver threads in a braid*

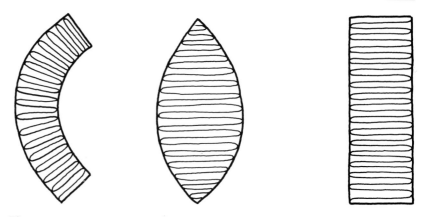

Fig. 23. *Weaver threads in differently shaped braids*

You will learn to determine yourself how many pairs to use in each motif. This comes with practice, trials and mistakes. The number of pairs depends on several factors. You can ask yourself:

- Which thread do I want to use?
- Is there a footside on one or either side?
- What is the result I want to achieve: thick solid-looking lace, or something more delicate?

Because you can determine these things yourself, you will find that you have a lot of freedom in expressing your own ideas, even when you use a pattern designed by someone else.

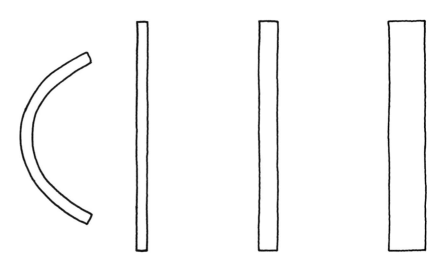

Fig. 24. *Some patterns of braids for practising*

Basic stitches

The basic stitches, which are half stitch and whole stitch, can each be worked in two methods. These two methods are called the open and the closed method. The open method is often used in Holland. This works faster, although the result is the same. Both methods are illustrated in fig. 25.

A different stitch is introduced when a plait or bar is made, and I shall explain this in the next chapter.

CLOSED METHOD

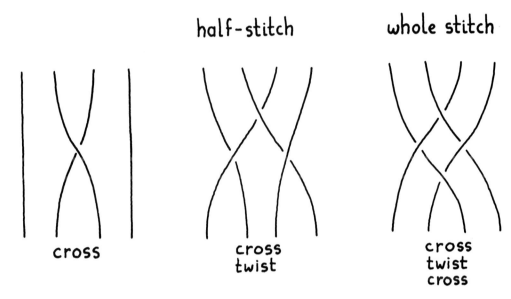

half-stitch   whole stitch

cross

cross
twist

cross
twist
cross

Fig. 25. *Basic stitches in open and closed method*

OPEN METHOD

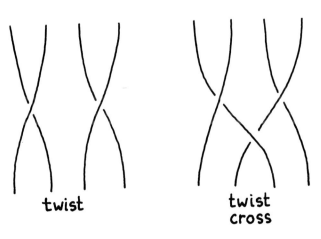
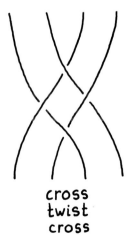

twist

twist
cross

cross
twist
cross

Footside

The footside in Duchesse is similar to the Torchon footside, and is worked with whole stitch and two or three twists. It is very important to twist at least twice because the footside holes are often used for sewings, and have to be strong on that account.

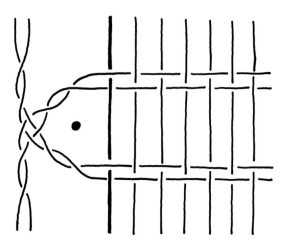

Fig. 26. *Duchesse footside*

Placing the pins

The basic rules of placing the pins are:

(*a*) Pins should be close to each other, but not overlap. When you press them down, the result should be a neat row of pinheads, not touching each other.

(*b*) The weaver threads should always be at right angles to the footside edge.

Setting up a braid (Fig. 27a–c)

For this sample use 8 pairs of bobbins. The technical way to indicate setting up with a certain number of bobbins is, for example, 4–2–2. This means that you hang 4 pairs on pin *A*, 2 pairs on pin *B* and 2 pairs on pin *C*.

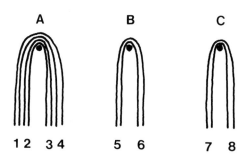

Fig. 27. *a–c Setting up a braid*

Work from left to right. This is usual, except in some cases, but these will be indicated.

With pairs 1 and 2 work whole stitch, twist twice.
With pairs 3 and 4 work whole stitch, twist twice.

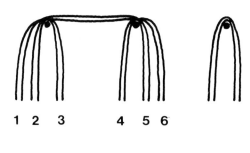

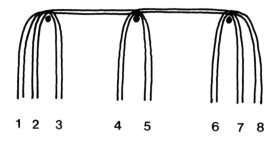

Do the same with pairs 4 and 5. Now hang pair 5 from left to right behind pin *B*, and put it back in its place, to the right of pair 4. With pairs 5 and 6 work whole stitch, twist twice. Do the same with pairs 6 and 7, and hang pair 7 around pin *C* in the same way as pair 5 was hung around pin *B*. With pairs 7 and 8 work whole stitch and two twists. The setting up is now completed and fig. 27c shows you what it should look like. This can of course be extended to more pairs, depending on how wide the braid is. For every two extra pairs, one extra pin is needed. The indication is then 4–2–2–2. If you have to set up starting from the right, you hang 4 pairs on the right-hand pin, and work from right to left.

Securing the threads and working the braid (fig. 28)

With the second pair from the left work whole stitch to the right until you come to the last pair. Put this and the weaver aside. With the pair on the left of the weaver work whole stitch to the left, until you come to the last pair. You now work the footside: twist twice and work whole stitch and two twists with the last pair. Work back to the right and there also work the footside in the same way.

Fig. 28. Securing threads at the beginning of the braid

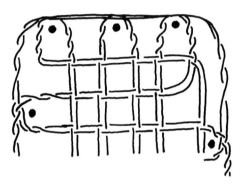

The gimp pair

The gimp is always the last thread before the footside, and always has a partner thread. These stay together. This means that when you work an area in half stitch, you *always* work through the gimp pair in whole stitch first. Then you twist the weaver pair and carry on in half stitch. When you come back to the footside you again work a whole stitch with the gimp pair.

Hanging in a gimp pair (fig. 29)

Knot one bobbin wound with a gimp to one bobbin wound with a thin thread. Secure the knot with a pin outside the pattern on the pillow.

After setting up the braid, before you come back to the left with the weaver, hang the gimp thread in the work as the 3rd from the left, and the thin thread as the 5th from the left. The thread to the right of the gimp becomes the partner. The hung-in thread becomes one of the passives. Work through these with the weaver coming from the right.

Fig. 29. *Hanging in a gimp pair*

Taking out a gimp pair

At the end of a motif or braid, the gimp pair can just be laid back and cut off later.

Curved braid

The important thing to keep in mind when you work a curved braid is that the line of the weavers should be horizontal on the vertical passives. This means that on the outside of the curve the pins will be put further apart than on the inside. It also means that on the inside from time to time a pin is not used. Work this as follows.

Work to the inside, but do not work the edge pair. Leave this and the weaver on one side. With the pair next to the weaver make a half knot and with this new pair work back to the outside. When you go back to the inside work the footside as usual.

Repeat this when necessary, perhaps after every 2 or 3 pins put on the outside.

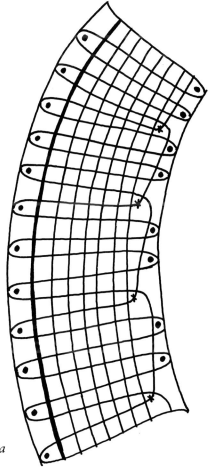

Fig. 30. *Diagram of a curved braid*

Adding pairs (fig. 31)

This way of adding new pairs can be used both in whole stitch and half stitch. Hang one pair round the last pin on the left, and lay this pair between the edge pair and the gimp thread. Work with this pair one half stitch to the right, so that the gimp thread is back in its place. Continue working. After you have set two or three more pins on the left remember to pull down the loop carefully, by taking the pin out, pulling the hung-in pair down and putting the pin back.

Fig. 31. *Adding pairs from a pin in the footside*

Adding a pair in a whole stitch area

Put a temporary pin in the place where the new pair has to be added, hang the new pair on this pin, and lay one new thread over the next old one to the left. Continue working, and after several rows, take out the pin and very carefully ease the threads down.

Fig. 32. *Adding pairs in a whole stitch area*

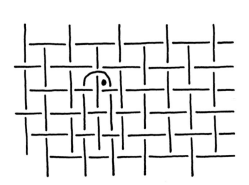

40

Taking pairs out

In whole stitch: work to the right. Lay back the 6th and 8th bobbin from the left. Repeat this as often as necessary. If you want to take out a number of pairs at once, lay back the bobbins with even numbers.

These threads are cut off close to the lace, when the piece is finished. It is unnecessary to knot them, as the whole stitch will keep them in place.

In half stitch: knot a non-adjoining pair (fig. 33) e.g. 4th and 6th threads, lay this pair back, and cut it off later.

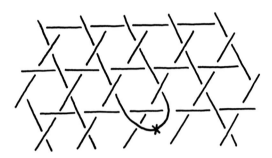

Fig. 33. *Taking out pairs*

Joining braids (fig. 34)

Work the footside stitch without twists. Sew the weaver pair into the nearest pinhole of the next braid.

Work another whole stitch with the footside pair, now twist twice and proceed to work back. Make sure the two braids are closely pulled together, with no loops showing. The number of times you sew in depends of course on the length of the edges to be joined.

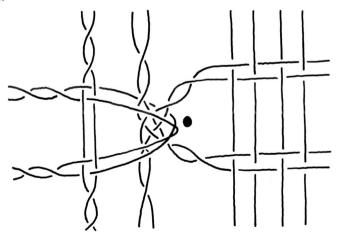

Fig. 34. *Joining braids*

Sewings

(a) *Ordinary*. Put the hook through the pinhole and pick up the thread through the hole, while you hold the bobbin in the other hand. Release the tension on the bobbin as soon as the hook comes back through the hole, and pull the thread through. Put the other weaver bobbin through the loop and pull tight. In some cases a knot can be necessary.

Fig. 35. *Ordinary sewing*

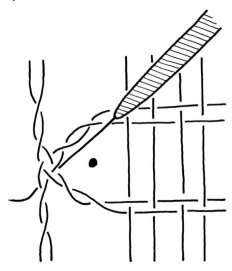

(b) *Raised*. Put the hook through the hole, but only around either the top or the bottom weaver-threads, not the footside edge threads as well. By doing this a ridge is created on the other side, which can look very effective. Be consistent in using either all top threads or bottom threads.

Sometimes you need to use all the top ones first, and when you use the same footside again, use all the bottom ones.

Fig. 36. *a, b Raised sewing. This leaves a 'rib' on the other side*

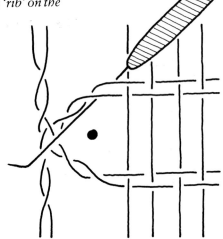
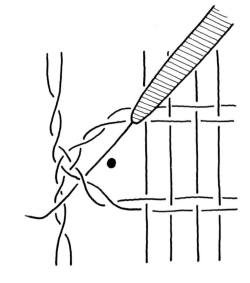

Sewing with a threaded needle

This is not a traditional Duchesse tool, but for many people it can be a very helpful one, so I shall explain how it is used. For most fine Duchesse work you will have to use a very thin needle, which is set into a wooden handle. The tool is often called a 'Lazy Susan'.

Thread approx. 20in (50cm) through the needle and knot it together at the end. Put the needle through the pinhole and pull half of the length of thread through to the other side. Pass the bobbin through this loop and pull it all back. Now take away the needle and thread and you have the loop ready to put the other bobbin through. Continue as for an ordinary sewing.

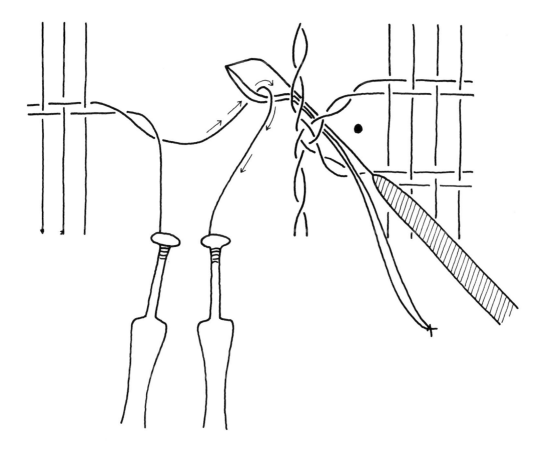

Fig. 37. *Sewing with a threaded needle*

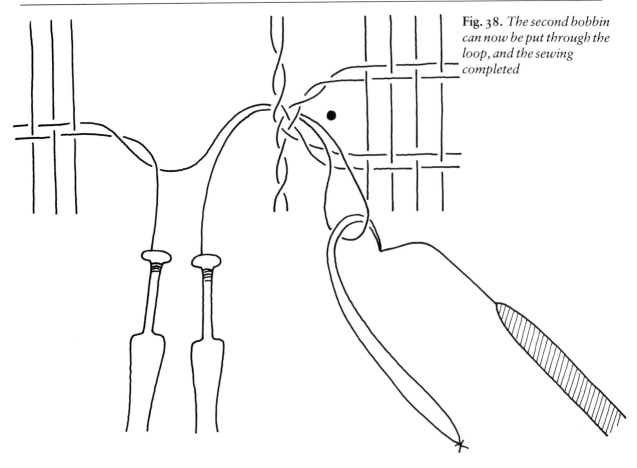

Fig. 38. *The second bobbin can now be put through the loop, and the sewing completed*

How to deal with a broken thread

One of the most common problems that occurs in lacemaking is that threads have a tendency to break. This happens especially when you have worked with thicker thread, and you are still getting used to a new thinner thread. Fortunately, although it is a nuisance, in Duchesse lace it is fairly easy to deal with. If the break happens in a tally, you will have to undo it and start again, but apart from this, there is no reason to worry too much. The one vital bit of knowledge you need is how to do a weavers' knot.

The weavers' knot is small and very firm, and is perfectly safe to use. Make sure that there is still about 1cm (³⁄₈in) of the broken thread hanging from the lace. With the new thread make a slip-knot (fig. 39), and put the end of the broken thread through the loop. Now take both ends of the slip-knot, making sure that the broken thread does not escape (this was when I discovered that thread has a mind of its own), and pull these, until the broken end is pulled through the loop, with a little 'click'.

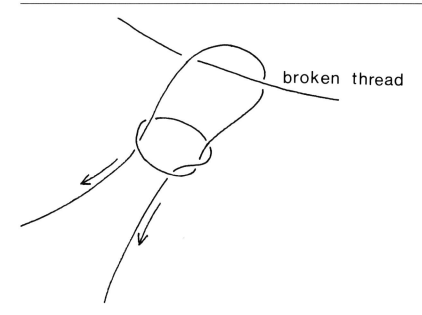

Fig. 39. *Weaver's knot*

broken thread

The way to check whether you have done it right, is to pull the broken end. It should stay where it is; if it doesn't, you may have to try again. If you practise this knot with a thicker thread, you will soon have no problems with it.

Apart from the tally, which I have mentioned, there is one other exception to using this knot. If the passive thread in a whole stitch area breaks, do not worry at all – just hang a new thread on a support pin outside the work, lay back the broken thread, and carry on working with the new thread. You can cut off the old and the new thread later. The whole stitch area will keep the threads in place.

If the break occurs in a half stitch area, undo the lace until the footside, so that you do not get a knot in the half stitch area.

4 Braids and connections

''Tis not the lip or eye we beauty call,
but the joint force and full result of all.'
Alexander Pope[12]

Braids

Braids can look like long thin pieces of bandage, or they can be
very decorative. There are several ways in which you can
achieve an effective result. I shall demonstrate some ways of doing
this, and I am sure you will experiment and find other ways too.

(*a*) One of the simplest decorations is achieved by giving the weaver
pair one or more twists in the middle of the braid, before you carry
on in whole stitch.

Fig. 40. *Practice pieces,*
mounted

(*b*) Instead of twisting the weaver pair, you might try making several half stitches. Remember to twist the weaver pair before you start the half stitches. Also make a note of how many pairs you work through before you start the half stitch. I have used this method in the lavender-bag edging, and in the body of the butterfly (fig. 129). The result is very effective and very simple.

(*c*) A more elaborate way of decorating a braid is by using two weavers. Coming from either side, they meet up in the middle. There you twist them both twice, work a cloth stitch and two twists, and then carry on, each one going his own way (fig. 41).

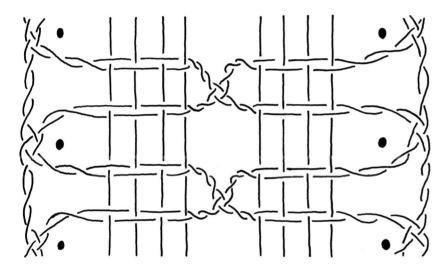

Fig. 41. *Braid with crossed weavers in the centre*

Fig. 42. *Working holes in cloth-stitch braid*

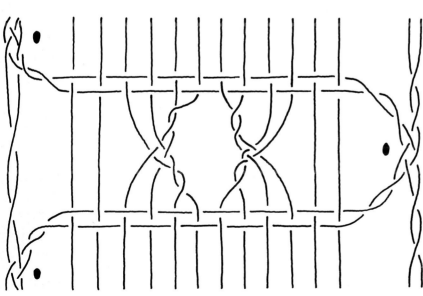

(*d*) Working holes into a braid looks very attractive. Only one weaver pair is necessary here. The weaver is still at the footside. Twist the two pairs in the centre of the braid twice. These work a whole stitch with their neighbour on either side. Again twist the middle two pairs twice. The weaver pair now works through all the pairs, and if you very gently pull the passives, you can get a beautiful round hole (fig. 43). It takes some practice, but the result is worthwhile.

Fig. 43. *Close-up of holes in a braid*

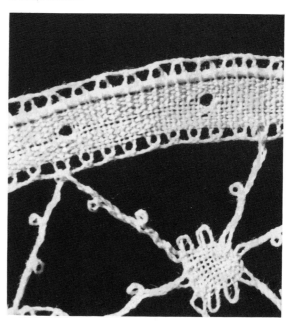

Fig. 44. *Braid with crossed weavers and pin in the centre*

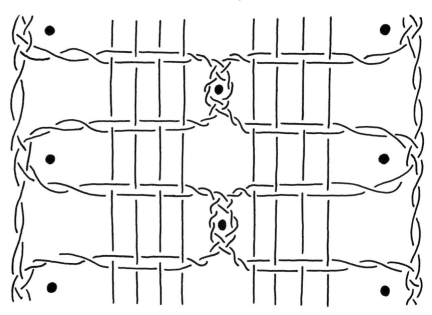

(*e*) Yet another possibility is to use a pin in the middle. Again there are two weavers. When they meet, you twist them both twice, work a whole stitch and twist, put a pin neatly in the middle, just below the level of both footside pins, and work another whole stitch and two twists. Each weaver carries on. Remember, a braid always looks best when the weavers are horizontal, and the passives vertical (fig. 44).

Picot edge

In Duchesse lace the outside edge of the lace is often decorated with picots. It gives the finished lace a romantic and delicate look, but that may not always be what you want. In the beautiful design of the fish (fig. 146) only the flowerhead is worked with picots and the rest is left with plain straight edges, in character with the texture of the fish. The result is very realistic. The picot edge is never used around the motif inside a piece of lace, except to decorate the connecting plaits.

You work the picot edge on the left as follows:

Work the footside stitch without the usual two twists. The outside pair is twisted 5 or more times – this depends on the thickness of the thread. Now put a pin underneath the left hand thread, pointing towards you, then up and over it towards the left away from you.

Fig. 46. *a–c Working a picot*

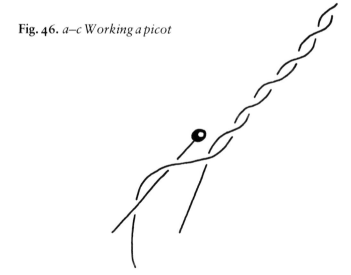

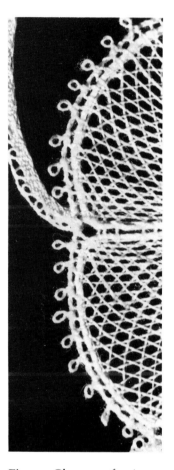

Fig. 45. *Close-up of a picot edge*

Put this pin on the outside line of the pattern you are working. Do not pull this thread yet, but take the second thread and let it follow the previous one in the same direction: away from you to the left, round the back of the pin to the right and towards you. Pull both threads gently, so that they are twisted firmly round each other and the pin, and twist twice.

49

Fig. 46. *b*

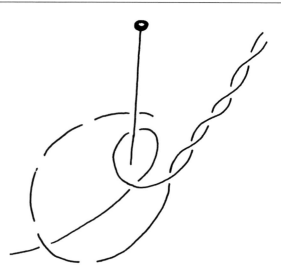

If you don't pull them enough, you may end up with a split picot, so it is important to:

(*a*) twist the threads often enough in the first place, before you make the picot.

Fig. 46. *c*

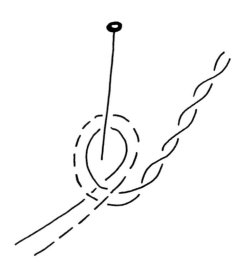

(*b*) make sure they are really twisted round each other before you finish.

Of course, if you pull too hard you may end up with a broken thread, so take care! Work a whole stitch with the footside pair, twist twice, and continue working. A picot to the right is worked the opposite way.

A corner in a braid

It is not usual to work a corner in Duchesse, as mostly the lines are rounded and flowing, but it is useful to know how to work one, in case you want to design your own patterns, and would like to include one.

There are several ways of working corners, but I shall give the one I prefer to use (fig. 47 & 48).

Fig. 47. *Working a corner*

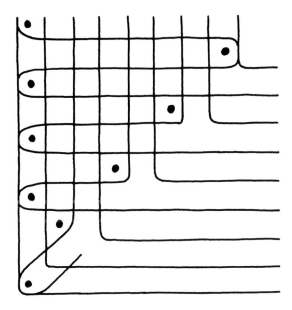

Fig. 48. *Completing a corner*

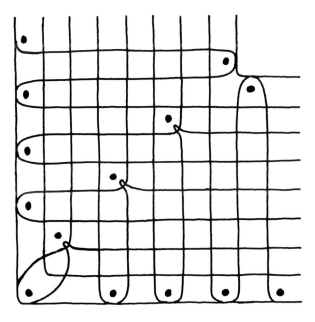

Fig. 49. *Corner, close-up*

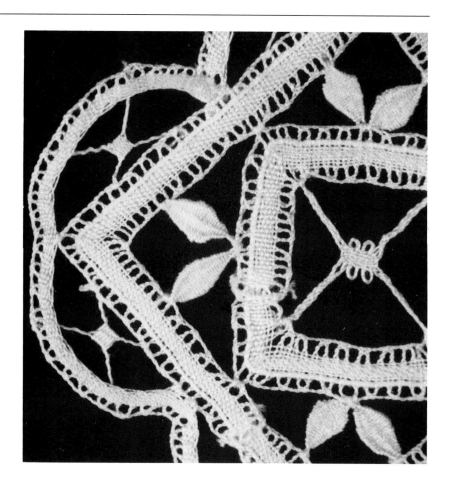

After working the last pin on the right, work to the left, and back to the right, until the footside pair, leave this and the weaver, plus the pair to its left. There are now three pairs waiting on the right. Take the next pair (4th from right), put a pin on the diagonal line to the left of the pair, and work to the footside and back. Leave it there, with the pair it has just worked through, and the three pairs already there. Take the next pair to the left (6th) and do the same. Continue until you have worked the corner pin. Now turn the pillow and take the weaver to the right in whole stitch until you reach the first pinhole. Sew the weaver pair in here and leave it, as a passive pair. Do not go back with this sewn-in pair to the footside, but take the pair to its right, and work to the left, through the sewn-in weaver. To the right again, sew into the next pinhole and leave it there. Take the pair to its right and continue in this way until you have used all the hanging pairs. Then make the footside stitch on the right and put a pin close to the corner. From now on continue with the braid as usual. Make sure you have spaced the pins out evenly, so that you will keep the weaver pair going horizontally.

Connections

The motifs and braids in Duchesse are linked together by bars, whole stitch blocks or tallies.

Fig. 50. *Working a plait*

Bars or plaits (fig. 50)

These are worked with two pairs and are used to connect different braids, flowers etc. Always start with a whole stitch, then twist, cross, twist, cross.

Plaits with picots (fig. 51)

(*a*) *Picots on left* After completing another twist, cross, you twist the left-hand pair 5–7 times and the right-hand pair twice. Work the picot itself as for the picot edge. After twisting the left-hand pair twice you work a whole stitch and continue with twist, cross, twist, cross.

(*b*) *Picots on right* After a cross, twist right-hand pair 5–7 times, and left-hand pair twice. Work the picot and twist right-hand pair twice. Continue with a whole stitch, and twist, cross.

Fig. 51. *Plaits decorated with picots*

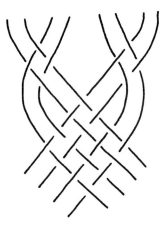

Crossing plaits (fig. 52)
Work both pairs of the left-hand plait in whole stitch to the right, then work a whole stitch with the two pairs that are now on the left, and a whole stitch with the two right-hand pairs. Continue working the plaits separately.

Tally

The Dutch word for tally is 'moesje' and in France it is called 'point de reprise'. It is one of the most difficult decorative stitches, since it demands great concentration and care, but the result is well worth the effort. Do not worry if you do not succeed at first. With practice you will quickly notice improvement!

The square tally appears in different types of lace, e.g. Torchon, Bucks Point, Honiton and Duchesse. In Duchesse the tally is often used to decorate small spaces, such as the centre of a flower, curl or berry (fig. 98). Sometimes larger areas are filled with rows of tallies (fig. 53).

Fig. 52. *Crossing plaits*

Fig. 53. *Close-up of tallies*

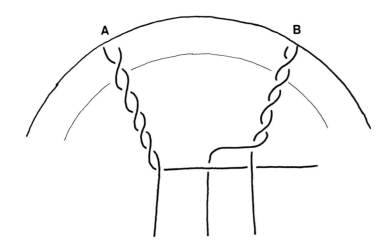

Fig. 54. *a,b. Working a tally*

The tally is worked with two pairs. These are hung in at *A* and *B* (fig. 54a). Twist each pair 6–8 times, depending on the space and the thickness of the thread. Take thread No. 2 and lengthen this. This is the weaver, and as it weaves through the other pairs to produce the square shape, it is important that you keep this thread longer than the others. It will make working much easier and the result will be better.

Hold the weaver in the same hand all the time, keeping it slack. Take it over thread No. 3 and under No. 4 to the right. At this stage it is essential that with your other hand you firmly hold the three passive bobbins, the outside ones slightly spread out. Then you can carefully pull the weaver up, so that the weaving thread closes up around the passive threads (fig. 54b). Weave back over 4, under 3, over and under 2, over 3 and under 4. Remember to keep the weaver slack and in the same hand. If you change it from hand to hand, it is all too easy to pull it by accident. Before you pull the weaver again, press the other three bobbins firmly down on the pillow, or hold

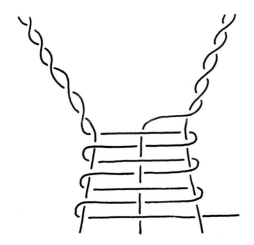

them firmly in your other hand. You can push the weaving thread upwards by pulling the outward passives away from each other.

If you pull the weaver too hard, loops will appear on the sides of the tally. If you pull the weaver without holding on to the other threads, the shape of the tally is lost and you might have to start again.

When the tally has the desired length, you leave the weaver on the right, and support it. I usually put a pin on each side of the bobbin, crosswise, so that it cannot move. Now take the first bobbin, and twist the second one around it, again 6 or 8 times. Sew this pair out at C and tie a reefknot.

Alternatively, tie a half knot and sew out again at the next pinhole with a reefknot there. Finish the second pair in the same way at D but try not to pull the weaver.

When you work a tally inside a rib, the result is better if you sew each pair into a pinhole at the outside of the rib, rather than through the threads on the inside (fig. 55).

Fig. 55. *Completing a tally*

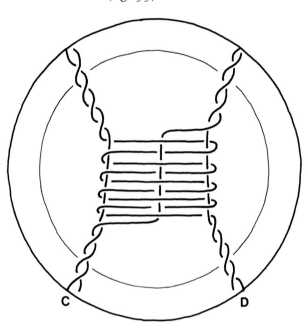

Fig. 56. *Leaf-shaped tally*

Tallies in the shape of a leaf

In some old Duchesse patterns in the collection of Mrs v.d. Meulen-Nulle, leaves can be seen as decoration usually as a filling, for example between two braids. It adds expression and charm to the finished work. Basically a leaf is worked like a tally, only you start and finish with a whole stitch. After that, the outside passives determine the shape, so the further they are held apart, the broader the leaf will become. Again, practice is essential as many find it difficult to obtain a good shape (Fig. 56).

When you have worked the leaf for two-thirds of the way, you begin to shape the end, by drawing the outside passives slightly together. Finish with a whole stitch, and make sure not to pull hard on the pair with the weaver when you continue working.

Whole stitch block with 4 pairs

This is a very effective way of crossing plaits. Fig. 57 shows a detailed diagram of how it is worked. The pairs are worked in plaits up to the block, and every pair twisted twice. Put up a pin between the two pairs of each plait. Take the pair on the extreme left and work through to the right in whole stitch. Leave it there. Take the pair to its left and work in whole stitch to the left. Twist 4 times, pin, and work back to the right through all pairs, twist 4 times, pin and back to the left. Repeat this. When you are back to the left, twist twice, put a pin and leave this pair on the left. Take the pair next to it and work to the right in whole stitch, twist twice, and put a pin.

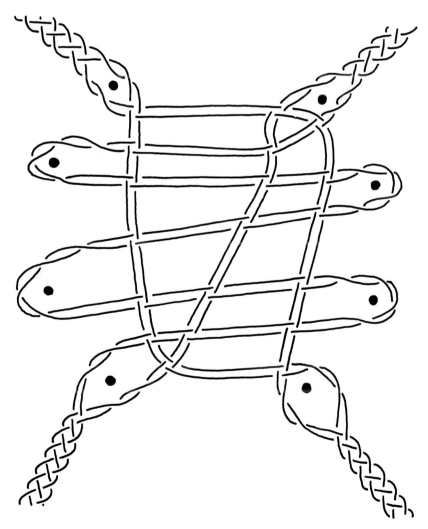

Fig. 57. *Whole-stitch block with 4 pairs*

Now twist the middle pairs twice. Join the left-hand pair with the outside pair on the left, and work a whole stitch to continue the plait. Do the same for the plait on the right-hand side.

Whole stitch block with 6 pairs (fig. 58)

This is a useful and decorative connection of three plaits.

Basically it is worked the same as the whole stitch block for 4 pairs.

Twist all pairs twice, and put a pin between the pairs of each plait. Work with the left-hand pair to the right in whole stitch. Leave this, and with the pair next to it work to the left. Twist 4 times, put a pin and work through all pairs back to the right. Twist 4 times, pin, and work back to the left. Repeat this. When the weaver is on the left again, twist twice, put a pin, and leave it. With the pair next to it work to the right, twist twice, and put a pin.

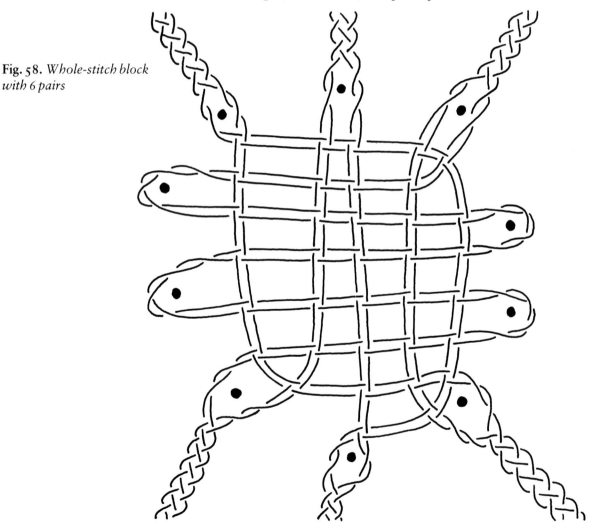

Fig. 58. *Whole-stitch block with 6 pairs*

With the pair next to this work to the left, but do not work the two pairs on the left. Twist twice, and put a pin in the middle. With the pair on its right, twist twice, and work a whole stitch to begin the middle plait.

Make sure all other pairs are twisted twice. With two pairs on the left work a whole stitch and start the plait on the left. Do the same with the two pairs on the right.

Continue working the three plaits.

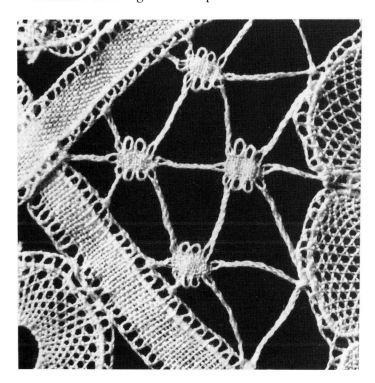

Fig. 59. *Whole-stitch blocks to fill a larger area*

Patterns (all worked in Egyptian cotton 100)

Small round or oval brooch (8 pairs + gimp pair)

Set up at A with 4–2–2. Hang in the gimp pair, and work the braid with picots on the outside. When the circle or oval is completed, finish off by sewing the pairs in each of the three starting pinholes.

Fill the centre with tallies or whole stitch blocks.

Fig. 61. *'Valerie', a round brooch with plaits and whole-stitch block*

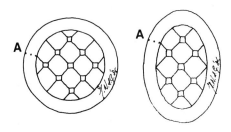

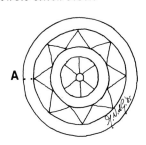

Fig. 60. *'Claudine', a round or oval brooch with picots and tallies*

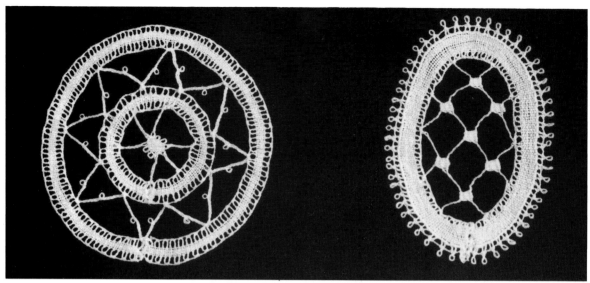

Fig. 62. *Round and oval brooch*

Round brooch (6 pairs + gimp pair)

Set up 4–2 at *A*. Hang in the gimp pair and work the braid. Finish off by sewing three pairs in each of the two starting pinholes.

Work the inside braid in the same way. Connect the two braids by hanging in two pairs at *A* and work the plaits from here all the way round. Work the whole-stitch block in the centre.

Star (12 pairs)

Start at the top with three false picots as follows: hang 2 pairs on each pin, twist the right-hand pair from each pin 7 times, and work

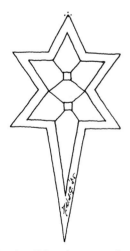

Fig. 63. *'Mary' pattern for star*

Fig. 64. *Star*

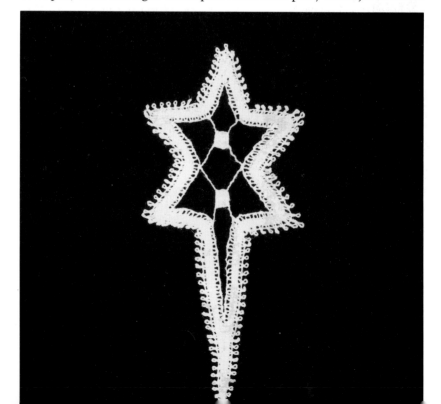

60

a whole stitch to enclose the pin. Hang two more pairs round the left-hand pin, and continue as if you were setting up from the beginning. Work the braid with picots on the outside. Add 4 more pairs and divide the braid to work the two separate ones.

The points are worked like corners. Towards the end of the lower point, the braids merge together, and you can lay pairs back as you work down, until you have only 4 pairs left at the end. These are knotted and cut off.

Square pattern (6 pairs + gimp pair)

First set up large square braid 4–2 with gimp pair. Work the small square, and join the corners to the large square. Work the rib (4–2) round the outside, joining at the corners and the sides of the square.

Lastly, work the leaves, tallies and whole-stitch block.

Fig. 66. *Square pattern*

Fig. 65. *'Leentje' square pattern with braid or rib on the outside (see chapter 5 for the working of the rib)*

5 Flowers and curls

'Where blooms the flower when her petals fade . . .'
Walter de la Mare[13]

Oone of the joys in Duchesse is the flower. There are many different shapes and sizes of flowers you can make. I shall give the instructions for a basic one, and give several ideas of how to make others. Basically it is up to you after that. Remember that to some extent they have to be simplified to be able to work them in lace, but there are so many possibilities when you have learnt the techniques, that simplifying and stylizing them is not really a limitation, but a challenge.

Fig. 67. *A lavender-bag*

The first one is a basic flower with five petals. On the inside of the flower is a small circle worked, called a rib. The rib has pins only on the outside. The inside shows a firm, neat line and this accentuates the appearance of the lace. Because there are pins only on the outside, there is only one circle drawn on the pattern (fig. 68).

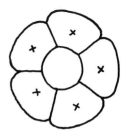

Fig. 68. *Flower with half-stitch petals*

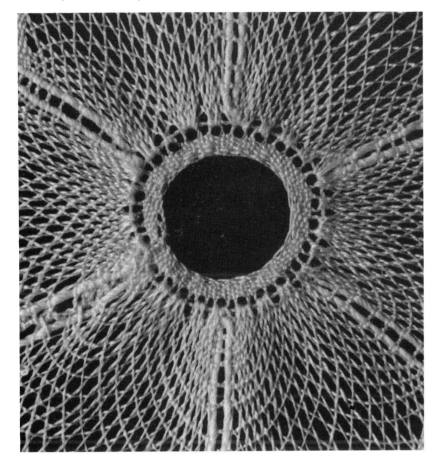

Fig. 69. *Close-up of rib inside flower*

The rib

Set up 4–2 on two pins. Put these close under the petal line, so that you can use the same bobbins that have worked the rib for working the petal. Hang four pairs on *A* and two on *B* (fig. 70). Set up as usual. Secure the threads by working to the right with the second pair. Do not work the last pair, but put this and the weaver pair to one side. Take the third pair from the right and work to the left. Put the footside pin on the circle. Work to the right through all pairs,

Fig. 70. *Starting-point for the rib*

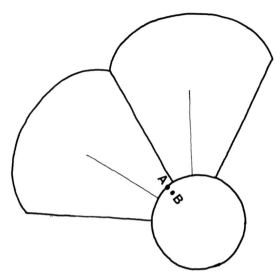

and leave the weaver. Take the pair to its left, and work back to the footside. Continue in this way (fig. 71).

Fig. 71. *Working the rib*

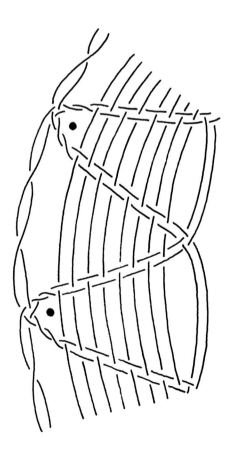

Closing the rib

The weaver is on the right (fig. 72). Take the pair on the left of the weaver through the pinhole at *B*, and take the weaver-pair through the loop. Pull tight. Work the weaver through all pairs to the left, and leave it there (fig. 73). Take the second pair through the pinhole at *A* and the third pair through the loop. Pull tight. You are now ready to start the first petal.

Fig. 72. *Closing the rib on the inside*

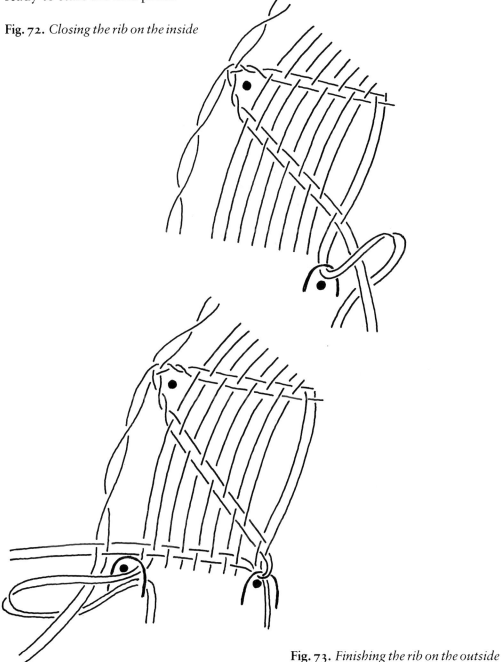

Fig. 73. *Finishing the rib on the outside*

Half-stitch petal

There are 6 pairs coming from the rib. First you hang in the gimp pair between the first and the second pair from the left (fig. 74). Take the pair on the extreme right, and work to the left in half stitch. Remember to work a whole stitch when you meet the gimp pair, work a footside stitch and put a pin on the line which divides the petals. Work back to the right, and put this pair on one side to the right.

Take the next pair, and work back to the left and to the right again. Leave this pair also. Take the next pair and do the same. There are now three pairs lying on the right (fig. 74). The 4th pair from the right is now the weaver, but it has to wait until you have added some more passive pairs.

The number of pairs depends on the size of the petal, and how closely woven you want it to be. There may be room on the dividing line for two or more pins, so you can put these in place. I personally think that it is better not to have too many pairs for half stitch, because a half-stitch area looks better when it is fairly open. Hang two pairs round each added pin (fig. 75). This time you set up from the right. Take the footside pair and work a whole stitch and two twists with the newly hung pair to its left. Hang the left-hand pair of these two round the back of the pin towards the left, and with this and the next pair work another whole stitch and two twists. Continue like this to the end.

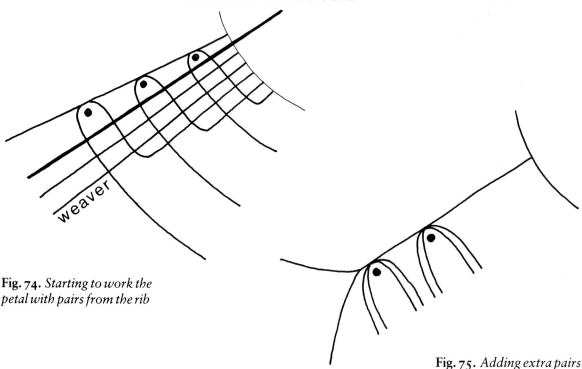

Fig. 74. *Starting to work the petal with pairs from the rib*

Fig. 75. *Adding extra pairs*

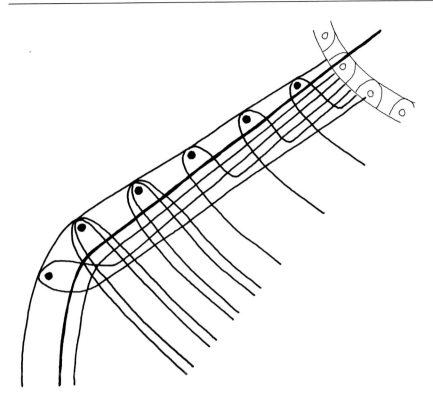

Fig. 76. *Working the petal*

The gimp pair will have to become the second pair from the left, so take this, and work whole stitch to the left, through all new pairs, until the footside pair (fig. 76). With the weaver (4th from the right) also work to the left, in half stitch, after you have twisted all new passive pairs once. Work the footside and put the pin on the rounded petal-edge. Work back to the right in half stitch, and sew into the first pinhole on the right. Then work back to the left. Continue working the footside on the left and sewing in on the right. Because the outside of the petal is rounded and larger than the inside, you may have to sew into the same pinhole two or three times. Try to space this evenly, so that the weaver threads are at right angles to the inner footside.

Dividing line between petals

When you have worked the last footside pin, leave the two footside pairs on the left. It is the gimp pair which makes the dividing line as follows: Take the gimp pair and work to the right through all pairs in whole stitch (fig. 77). Sew the thin thread into the pinhole, and take the gimp through the loop. Make a half knot with the thin thread on top of the gimp-thread, so that it stays in place.

Twist all passive pairs twice (not the two footside pairs) and work

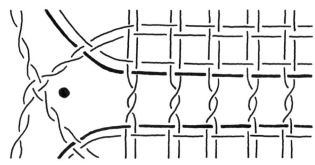

Fig. 77. *Working the division between the petals*

Fig. 78. *Division between petals*

back to the left in whole stitch with the gimp pair, until the last footside pair. Do not set a pin. Twist all passive pairs once, so that they are ready for the next half-stitch area, and work to the right with the weaver -pair. From here work the second petal like the first one.

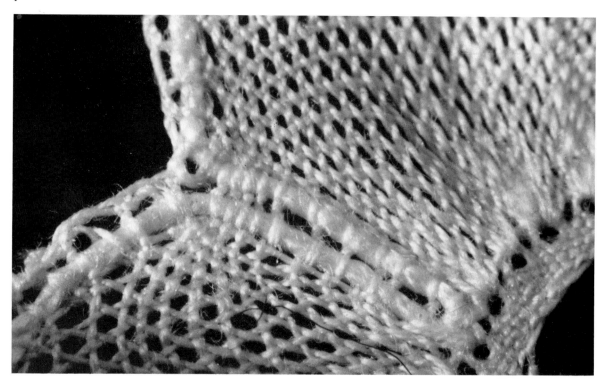

Finishing the flower

When you have worked the last petal, take the gimp pair to the right in whole stitch and sew in. Knot it and lay this pair back, to be cut off later. All the passive pairs are twisted twice. You will probably have to sew in two pairs at each pinhole, so divide them evenly. When you sew in two pairs into one hole, hook one pair through the pinhole, and take the other pair through the loop. Take one thread of each of the two pairs and make a reefknot.

Different petals (fig. 79)

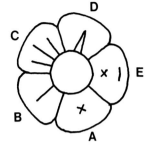

(a) Half-stitch petal

(b) Whole-stitch petal The whole-stitch petal is worked like the half-stitch petal. It is very important to make sure that the passive pairs follow an even line, so that the threads are evenly spaced vertically. Especially on the rounded outside of the petal, the threads should follow the outer line.

Fig. 79. *Different petals*

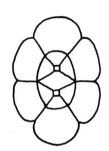

Fig. 80. *a,b. Practice patterns for flowers*

(c) Whole-stitch petal with three divisions The weaver is on the left. Leave about four pairs on the left, then twist the others twice, all the way to the inner edge. Do this three times evenly spaced in the petal.

(d) One division with pins (fig. 81) The weaver is on the left. Leave one passive pair on the inside. Take the next two pairs, twist them twice, put a pin between them on the top line, work a whole stitch, twist twice again, and put a pin between them on the bottom line. Do this with the next pairs. Make sure several pairs on the outside are left untouched. Now take the weaver, and work to the right through the unworked passives. Twist three times, put a pin on the point at C, and work back to the outside edge. Continue working the petal as usual from here.

(e) Half-stitch petal with whole-stitch outline Work three or four whole stitches after the gimp, then carry on into the petal in half stitch. Make sure you work the same number of whole stitches in each row.

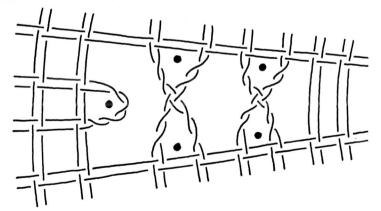

Fig. 81. *Using pins to decorate a petal*

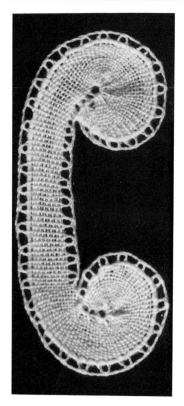

Fig. 82. *Curl, method 1*

Fig. 83. *Working the curl at the beginning of a braid, method 1*

The curl

There are several ways of working a curl. I shall give two different methods, of which I personally prefer the second, as it is more fun to work. Much depends on the result you want to aim for. The first one is worked more closely, whereas the second one gives a more open effect.

Method 1

Set up 4 pairs on *B*, and 2 pairs on *A* (fig. 83). After securing the threads as usual, hang in the gimp pair before working the first footside stitch on the left, and one extra pair. Make the footside stitch at *C*, return to *A* through all the pairs and leave the weaver there. Work back to the left with the next pair. Before you reach the gimp pair, add one more extra pair, and then work the footside pin at *D*. When you tighten the threads make sure that you pull the second pair from the right towards the right, so that there will be no gap in the centre.

Work back to the right through all pairs and sew in at *A*. Put the pin back and return to the left, adding another pair before you work *E*. Repeat in this way – one row without sewing in, the next row sewing in at *A*. You may have to add more pairs, this depends on the thickness of threads you are using. (Remember to pull down the loops of the pairs that have been added.) Continue until you reach *F*. Sew in at *A* once more, then from *G* sew in at *B*. Now the curl itself is completed. At *H* you work a second footside. When you reach the last pair twist this and the weaver twice. Work a whole stitch and two twists, and put a pin on the line at *H*, inside the two pairs. Continue working the braid with a footside on both sides.

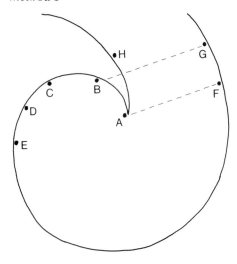

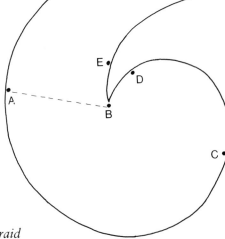

Fig. 84. *Finishing a braid with a curl, method 1*

Finishing the braid with a curl (method 1, fig. 84)

Work the braid until A and B. From then on work one row, sewing in at B, and one row without sewing in, like at the beginning of the curl. After you have worked the footside at C, remember to lay back one pair each time. When you have put the pin at D, you should have 5 pairs left. Work to B, and sew in the two right-hand pairs. Lay back the gimp pair and sew in the two remaining pairs at E.

Method 2

Set up 4 on B and 2 on A. After securing the threads and before you work to the left, hang an extra pair on B, and hang in the gimp pair. Work the footside pin at C and work back to the right. Leave the weaver there. Hang another extra pair on pin at C. Now take the 5th pair from the left, and work to the footside at D. Back to the right, and leave the weaver. The pairs marked W are going to be weavers, while the gimp pair and the two pairs to its right (marked P) will stay passives. There are three more pairs to be worked as weavers. Since the last footside pin for these three pairs should be straight underneath A, the pins should be spaced out evenly. Continue taking the 5th pair from the left, working to the footside and back, and leaving it out.

When you have worked the footside at E, turn the pillow, so that E is on your left, and work to the right through *all* pairs (fig. 87). Leave the weaver. Again, take the 5th pair, work the next footside pin, back to the right, and leave the weaver with the one already there. You will notice that you are working the same sequence as before. Pin F should be underneath pin A, so take care to space the pins evenly again. When you have worked pin F, take the weaver to the right and this time sew in at A (fig. 87). Work back to the

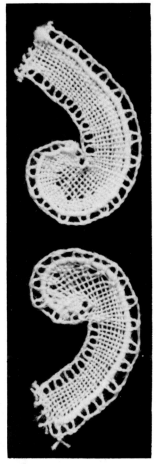

Fig. 85. *Curl, method 2. The curl at the top has more passive pairs, and looks fuller*

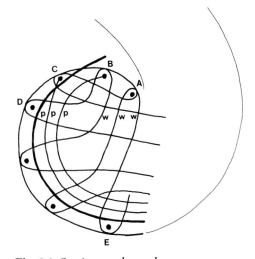

Fig. 86. *Setting up the curl*

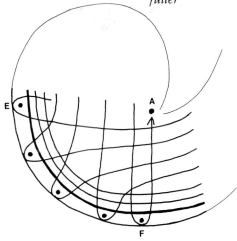

Fig. 87. *Working the curl*

Fig. 88. *Working the curl and the braid*

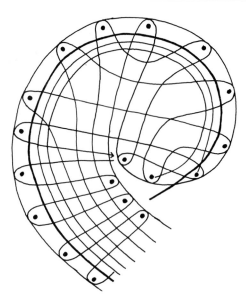

Fig. 89. *Practice pattern for curl*

footside on the left, and back to the right. Do not work the last pair, but twist this and the weaver twice. Put the footside pin on the line underneath *A*, and continue working the braid with a footside on both sides (fig. 88).

Finishing the braid with a curl (method 2, fig. 90)
After the footside pin at *A*, work to the right, and leave the weaver. Take the 5th pair, work to the footside and back to the right, leave the weaver. Continue like this, spacing out the pins evenly, until you have worked the footside pin at *B*. Turn the pillow, so that *B* is on your left (fig. 91). Work to the right through *all* pairs and leave the weaver. When you have worked the footside pin at *C*, work again through all pairs, and sew in at *D*. Lay back the gimp pair, and the even numbered threads. Work back to *E*, and again back to *D*, and sew in the weaver pair with the last passive pair. Knot these, and the other two remaining pairs and cut off.

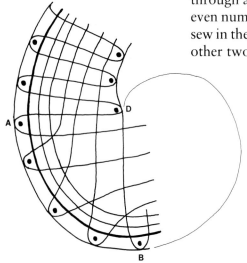

Fig. 90. *Finishing a braid with a curl, method 2*

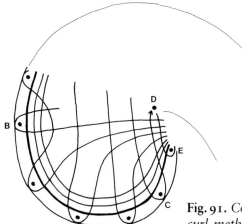

Fig. 91. *Completing the curl, method 2*

'Beads on a string'

There are basically two ways of working this attractive feature of Duchesse. The 'beads' can be round or oval, and can be used effectively in designing (figs. 140 and 144).

Method 1

Rib on the outside, filled with half stitch, or left open (fig. 92). Set up as for a rib at A. Work the rib in the direction of the arrow, with pins on the left, until B. From here the pins have to be set on the right. When you have put the pin at B, work to the right as usual, but with the last pair on the right work a whole stitch and two twists. Put a pin inside these two pairs at C, work to the left in whole stitch and leave the weaver. Work the rib to D with the pins on the right, and then change again to working the pins on the left. Work all round like this until you come back to E.

Sew in at the pinhole on the right of the previous rib, work to the left, and sew in at the pinhole on the left. With the pinholes on the left continue this braid until the next crossing at D. Do the same here, sewing in first on the left and then on the right. Work the next part of the rib with the pinholes on the right. When you come back to A, finish off the rib.

If you choose to fill the beads with half stitch you can use these pairs to work down in half stitch, sewing in each time in the pinholes on the outside of the rib. Make sure the weaver thread is horizontal. If you decide to leave the beads open, you can knot the threads firmly, and cut them off.

Method 2

Half stitch beads with gimp on the outside (fig. 98). Set up on the top with 4–2–2. When you have set up, take a double gimp pair (one pair with gimp thread, the other pair with thin thread) and work this in whole stitch through all pairs except the outside pair on each side (fig. 93). Now take the third pair from the left, and secure the threads in the usual way, in half stitch. Work the bead in half stitch (whole stitch with the gimp pair) and a footside on both sides.

When you come to the division, set the last pin on the left, and leave the two footside pairs there. Take the left-hand-side gimp pair

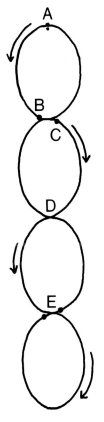

Fig. 92. *Working the beads, method 1*

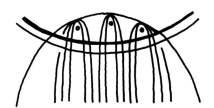

Fig. 93. *Setting up the beads, method 2*

73

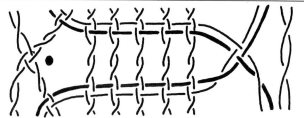

Fig. 94. *Working the division between the beads, method 2*

to the right in whole stitch. Cross it with the other gimp pair, and twist all passive pairs twice (fig. 94). Cross the gimps with their partner-threads, because the gimp should be on the outside of the work, and the thin thread on the inside.

Take the other gimp pair to the left in whole stitch. Twist all the passive pairs once, so that they are ready for the next half-stitch section, and work to the right with the footside pair.

To finish, work with the gimp pair to the right. Cross all passive pairs twice. Work to the right with the footside pair. Knot all pairs and cut off.

Flower with five petals
(9 pairs and 1 gimp pair)

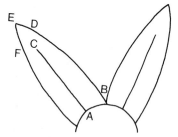

Fig. 95. *Directions for working the flower*

Work the centre rib as usual, setting up with 4–2, but start in line with the centre line of the petal (fig. 95). This will make working the petal easier later on, as you can use the pairs from the rib for this. After finishing the rib, work whole stitch and two twists with the two right-hand pairs, and put a pin on the centre line, inside these two pairs. Hang in two more pairs, and the gimp pair. Work to the left in whole stitch and put a pin on the footside at B. Continue until C and D.

Now work from the left in whole stitch through all pairs, including the footside pair on the right. Leave the weaver, and use the next pair to work back to the left. Work again to the right through all pairs, including the one which was left out, and now sew into the pinhole at C. Continue like this until you have worked pin E, alternately sewing in at C, and leaving the weaver. The second half of the petal is worked in half stitch, and to get a more open effect, you will need fewer pairs. Lay back 2 or 4 even-numbered bobbins. Twist all passive pairs once, and work from the footside to pin C in half stitch. Sew in here. Keep working in half stitch, sewing in at C until you have reached F. From here sew in at each next pinhole on the centre line. When you have sewn in at the last pinhole on the centre line, sew the last two pairs in again at the nearest pinhole of the rib. Leave one pair here, and work to the left with the other pair, but do not work the gimp pair and the footside pair.

Leave the weaver with these two pairs. With the pair on its right work to the right and sew in at the next pinhole of the rib. Work to the left, and leave the weaver pair with the others already there.

Take the next pair, work to the right, and sew in at the next pinhole. Now work back to the left until you come to the gimp pair. To keep this in place work the following sequence: 2 over 3, 2 and 4 over 1 and 3, 2 over 1, 2 over 3. The gimp pair should be back in its own place, and it is held tight by the weaver pair. Work back to the right and sew in at the next pinhole. Work to the left but do not work the gimp pair and the footside pair. Leave the weaver with these, and take the pair next to them to work back to the right. You may have to do this once more, until you have sewn in at the last pinhole nearest to the centre line of the next petal. Now work a whole stitch and two twists with the last two pairs on the right, and put a pin on the centre line of the petal. Continue working this petal in the same way as the previous one.

To finish off, lay the gimp pair back, sew the other pairs into the pinholes of the rib, and cut off.

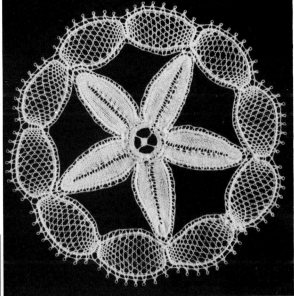

Fig. 98. *Flower and beads*

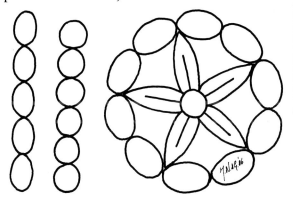

Fig. 96. *Practice pattern for beads* **Fig. 97.** *Pattern for flower and beads*

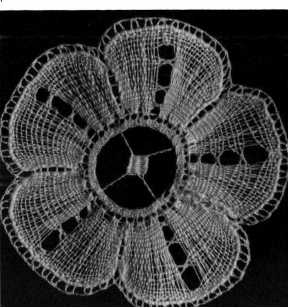

Fig. 99. *Round flower with 5 petals and division with pins*

Fig. 100. *Oval flower*

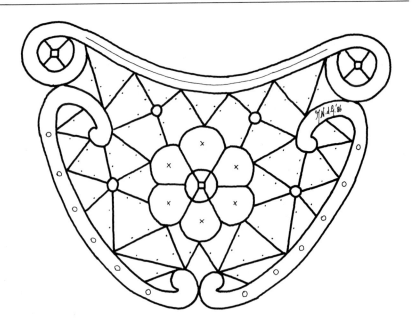

Fig. 101. *'Marieke', pattern for a pocket-decoration*

Patterns

Pocket decoration (Brok cotton 100 – maximum 11 pairs)

Start with the top braid, setting up at *A* with 4–2–2 + gimp pair. Work the decoration by twisting the weaver 3 times.

Work the side braids, beginning at the top curl, setting up 4–2. Increase to 11 pairs + gimp-pair. Work the holes in the braids as indicated.

Work the centre flower.

Lastly, decorate the open spaces with bars and picots, whole-stitch blocks and tallies.

Lavender bag (Egyptian cotton 100 – maximum 11 pairs)

Work the 4 outside braids, setting up 4–2 for the curl. Add the gimp pair, and 4 extra pairs.

Scallop-edge (10 pairs + gimp-pair)

To set up, sew 4 pairs into the curl at *A* (fig. 103), and hang 2 pairs on 3 pins between the curl and the braid. Set up as usual from the left. Before securing the threads from the left, take the gimp-pair through all pairs from the right, except the footside pair. Work the edge with a footside on the left, and sewing in on the right, like the flower-petals.

Fig. 102. 'Marieke', a
pocket-decoration

Fig. 103. 'Jean', pattern for a lavender bag

Fig. 104. 'Jean', lavender bag

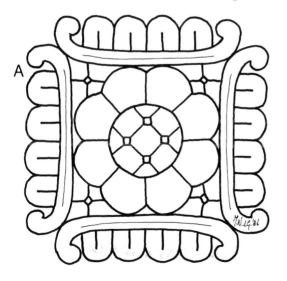

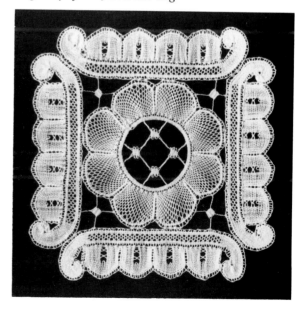

Finishing off:
You can work the gimp pair to the right and finish the passives in the usual way, but there is a different way of doing this. It is slightly more complicated, but it does mean that all the passive pairs are worked in, and the end will look as neat as the beginning.

Fig. 105. *Finishing the lavender bag edging*

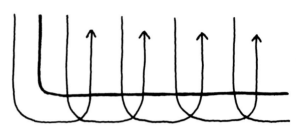

The weaver pair is on the left, together with the footside pair. Work the footside stitch without putting a pin. Now take the gimp pair, and work one whole stitch to the right. Twist the pair now on the left of the gimp pair twice, and work a whole stitch with the pair on its left.

Take one of the pairs on the extreme left, sew it into the pinhole of the curl, and take the other one through the loop. Knot these two pairs firmly, and lay aside, to be cut off later.

There is now 1 pair on the left of the gimp (fig. 105). Take the pair to the right of the gimp pair and work a whole stitch to the left. Twist twice and work a whole stitch and 2 twists with left-hand pair. Work the right-hand pair of these two to the right through the gimp pair, and lay it back, to be knotted and cut off later. Repeat from.

Put a footside pin after every two pairs. The best time is before you make the whole stitch and two twists with the pair on the left.

The last two pairs are sewn into the footside of the braid on the right, knotted and cut off.

Flower (11 pairs):
Work as usual and join the petals to the braid on all sides. Last of all, work the tallies in the open spaces.

6 Leaves, fillings and berries

'Cowslips and daisies, buttercups, and crowds without a name as if they dropt from clouds.'

John Clare[14]

When you study old Duchesse lace, you will find that there are different types of leaves. I shall show you how to work the most common of these, and I do recommend you to study old lace, so that you will discover varieties that you might like to try out for yourself. I will start with what, on the Continent, is called a cloverleaf.

Fig. 106. *'Mattie', a bookmark*

Fig. 107. *Practice pattern of the cloverleaf*

Cloverleaf (10 pairs + gimp pair)

Set up either from a curl or in a straight braid, with a gimp pair on the left and work the stem until pin *A* on the left (fig. 108*a*). Work the rounding on the right, while you sew in on the left in *A*. Do not work the footside pair. This can be left hanging until later. After the pin at *B*, sew in once more, and put a pin on *C*. Turn your pillow round and work from *C* to the left in whole stitch. You may have to sew in at *A* once more. After this, add 4 more pairs, while you continue to *D*. Remember to pull down the loops.

On the outside the pins should be slightly further apart, so that *E* and *D* are in line (fig. 108*b*). Now work from left to right in whole stitch, through all pairs, including the footside pair. Leave the weaver, and return with the next pair. Work again to the right through all pairs, including the one which was left, and now sew into pinhole at *D*. Continue like this until you have worked pin *F*.

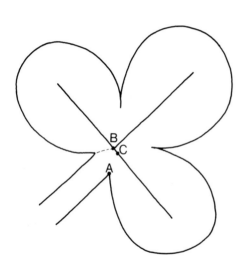

Fig. 108. *a. Starting the cloverleaf*

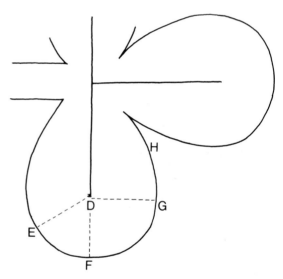

Fig. 108. *b. Working the cloverleaf*

The second half of this leaf is worked in half stitch, so you will need fewer pairs. Lay back 4 even-numbered bobbins. Twist all pairs once, and work from the footside to pin *D* in half stitch. Sew in here. Keep working in half stitch, sewing in at *D* until you have worked *G*. Then sew in at each next pinhole on the centre line. Do this until you have reached *H*. You will have to lose several pairs now. I usually do this in the following way: work with the weaver to the centre through all pairs (still in half stitch) and put it away to the right. (fig. 108*c*). Sew the next passive pair into the centre pinhole, and work back to the footside with this pair. Knot the pair that was put on one side, so that you can cut it off later. Repeat this

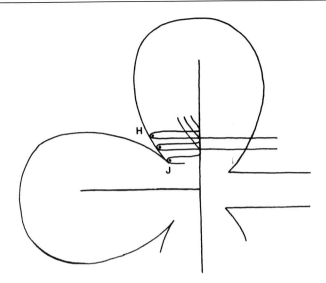

Fig. 108. *c. Reducing pairs at the end of a cloverleaf*

procedure two or three times. Change to whole stitch. Use the pinhole at *J* several times for sewing in until you have put the first pin on the centre line for the next leaf. Work the second leaf in the same way as the first one, adding the pairs that you took out.

At the end of the last leaf reduce the number of pairs as before, until you have four pairs left over. Sew out two pairs at the centre, and the other two in a pinhole of the stem. If any more pairs are left, they can be knotted together and cut off.

Fig. 109. *Cloverleaf*

Fillings (fig. 110)

Whereas in Honiton lace fillings are a very important and prominent feature, this is not so in Duchesse. Even so, open spaces in Duchesse lace can be filled in different ways.

1. A small space is usually filled with a tally.
2. A narrow strip can be filled with a row of tallies, or whole stitch blocks. Small leaf-shaped tallies look very effective, but a much simpler way is using bars decorated with picots.
3. Larger spaces need more substantial fillings. A few examples are point ground (half stitch and 2 twists), Torchon double ground (whole stitch and twist, pin, whole stitch and 2 twists), squares (whole stitch and 4 twists, no pins), half-stitch ground.
4. For very large spaces, it is effective to use bars, picots and whole-stitch blocks.

Fig. 110. *Different fillings*

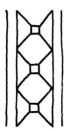  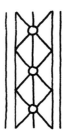  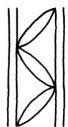

Berries (fig. 112)

There are several ways in which a berry can be worked. I shall give the main differences in the order in which they are placed on the photograph. All these have been worked in 100 cotton, and the number of pairs varies.

1. Work a braid in whole stitch, and fill in with a tally.

2. Set up 4–2–2–2–2 and a gimp pair (you can of course set up with fewer pairs if you use a thicker thread).

Fig. 111. *Patterns for berries*

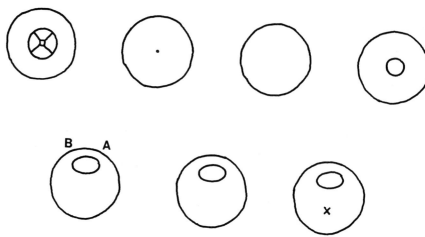

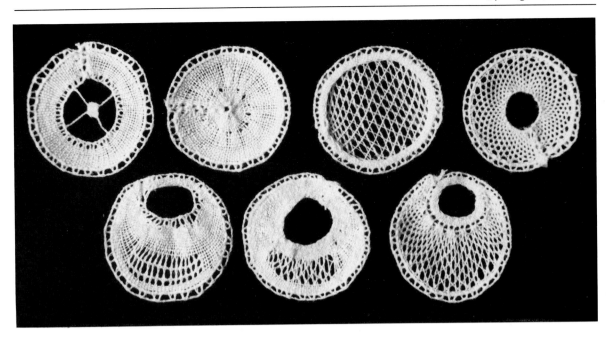

First row: work to the centre in whole stitch. Leave the weaver. Work back to the left with the next pair.

Second row: work to inner circle. Put a pin on the left of the weaver and the last pair worked. Go back with this pair.

Third row: work to the centre and sew in.

Fourth row: work to the centre and leave the weaver. Work back with the next passive pair.

Fifth row: work to inner circle. Take out the previous pin, and put in the next support pin as before. Repeat the last three rows.

3. Work a rib on the outside of the berry, then fill in with a half-stitch ground.

4. Put 4 or 5 support pins on the inner circle, leaning slightly outward, and wind some thread around it several times, then knot it firmly. Set up 4–2–2 and a gimp pair, and work in half stitch, sewing in at the centre circle each time.

5. Work a rib from *A* to *B*. Carry on working in whole stitch and add pairs as necessary. Work two rows with a pin and two rows without as follows: work to the inside until the last pair, put this and the weaver on one side. Take the third pair from the right, and put a pin to its left, to keep it in place. Then work to the left and back to the right until you reach the last pair (this was left out before). Put this and the weaver aside. Take the next pair and work to the left. Now work two rows with a footside pin on the right, and take out the support pin.

The sequence is: twice to the right with only one support pin;
twice to the right with footside pins.

Fig. 112. *Berries, differently worked*

As you get nearer to the end, remember to lay back the pairs that were added. After you have put the last pin on the left, lay back the gimp pair, and work to the right. Six pairs are left. Sew out three pairs at *B*, and three at *A*.

6. This berry is worked without any pins on the inside. Set up 4–2–2 + gimp. Work with the footside on the outside, but leave the weaver on the inside, as when you work a rib. Bring in more pairs as necessary. The example was worked with 14 pairs in total. When you start the half-stitch decoration, work three whole stitches from the footside, then two half stitches, and whole stitch again. Continue working these half stitches in every row, in the same place.

7. Work a rib on the inside, then set up and work in half stitch or whole stitch, sewing into the pinholes of the rib. You will have to sew in more than once into each pinhole.

Leaves starting at a point (fig. 113)

Hang 4 pairs on pin *A* and 2 pairs on both *B* and *C*. Setting up starts from the middle. Take the two left-hand pairs hanging from pin *A* and work whole stitch and two twists. Work to the left. With the right-hand pair from *B* work a whole stitch and two twists. Hang the left-hand pair round the pin and work whole stitch and two twists with the last pair.

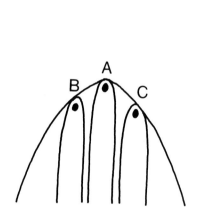

Fig. 113. *Setting up for a leaf, starting at a point*

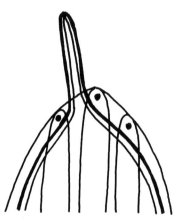

Fig. 114. *Hanging in the gimp pair*

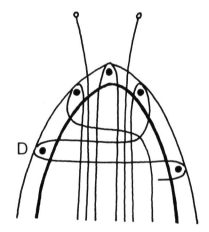

Fig. 115. *Securing the threads and adding extra pairs*

Do the same with the two right-hand pairs from *A* towards the right. Hang a double gimp pair (2 bobbins with gimp, 2 with thin thread) on a support pin. Work this through all pairs except those on the outside (fig. 114). You may need to hang in some extra pairs straight away (fig. 115). Now take the third pair from the left, and work to the right until you reach the last two pairs. Leave it there.

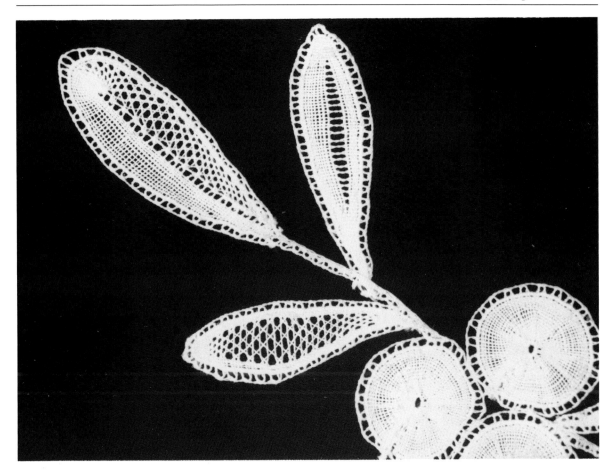

Take the pair to its left and work to the footside at *D*. Work the rest of the leaf, and add pairs if necessary.

Leaves started from a rib (fig. 117)

Work a rib from *A* to *B*. Here hang in more pairs and the gimp pair. Make a second footside on the centre line (whole stitch and two twists with the two right-hand pairs, and a pin inside these two on the centre line). Work the leaf like a cloverleaf, setting the pins on the outside slightly further apart than on the inside. Change to half stitch when you reach *C*, laying out two or three pairs. Begin to reduce pairs to the right when you reach *D*, as in the cloverleaf, so that you finish with a minimal number of pairs. This makes finishing off more tidy.

Fig. 116. *Different leaves. The outside two have been started at a point. The middle one was worked from a rib*

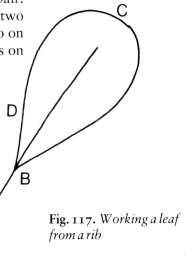

Fig. 117. *Working a leaf from a rib*

85

Leaf with rolled edges, without gimp
(11 pairs, figs. 118 and 119)

Start at point *A* with 2–4–2 pairs (fig. 119), but do not hang in a gimp pair this time. Hang in 3 extra pairs. As you work down to *B*, lay back 4 pairs, so that there are 7 left over. When you have put in the last pin, work to the left through all pairs in whole stitch. Turn the pillow, and sew into the pinhole that was last used, at *B*. Put one of the threads of the weaver pair underneath the bundle away from the footside, and the other weaver thread over the top (fig. 120). Cross these threads, and take them back, one over, one under.

Sew into the next pinhole. Continue like this until you have reached *C*. After you have sewn in here, put the weaver pair once more round the bundle, and sew in again into the same pinhole. This will hold the threads tightly against the top of the leaf. Now try and create some order in the bundle, and make a footside stitch (whole stitch and two twists) with the weaver pair and the pair next to it, and put a footside pin on the line of the top of the leaf. Work a rib until point *D*.

Fig. 118. *Numbering the leaves to show the order of working*

Fig. 119. *Starting the leaf*

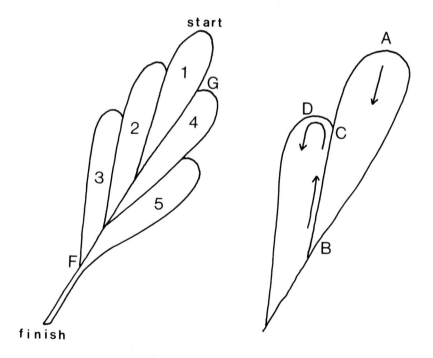

Note: If the leaf is very narrow, and only a few pairs are needed, work the rib, but leave the weaver hanging out on the inside of the rib each time, without using it again, so that it becomes a passive pair. This spaces out the pairs evenly.

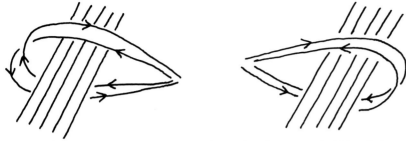

Fig. 120. *a. Tying the bundle of threads on the left of the footside*

Fig. 120. *b. Tying the threads on the right of the footside*

Hang in some more pairs. I use the pairs that were laid back from the previous leaf, by guiding them round a support pin outside the work. This saves time and at the end of the work you can just cut off all the loose threads. Work this leaf with the new footside on the left, and sewing into the pinholes on the right, using the lower threads (fig. 36a and b).

To cover the rounded top of the leaf you might have to sew into the same pinhole twice to begin with, so that you do not get any ugly holes. With some practice you will know how to avoid this.

When you have used the last pinhole on the right at B, make a footside stitch with the two right-hand pairs, and put a pin inside these two pairs on the line just underneath the one you have just used. From here work the rest of this leaf with a footside on each side. Lay back pairs as the leaf gets narrower, until you have 7 pairs left over. Work the next leaf like the previous one.

When you have reached F (fig. 118), work through all pairs to the right, and sew in at the last pinhole. Turn the pillow and lay all the pairs alongside the centre line. Cross the weaver pair over and under the bundle and sew into the pinholes on the right, all the way to G. Work leaf no. 4 like the other ones, only this time the footside is on the right, and you sew in on the left, using the top holes (fig. 36a).

At the end of the last leaf, reduce the pairs until 6 are left, and work a rib to finish.

Fig. 121. *Leaf with rolled edges*

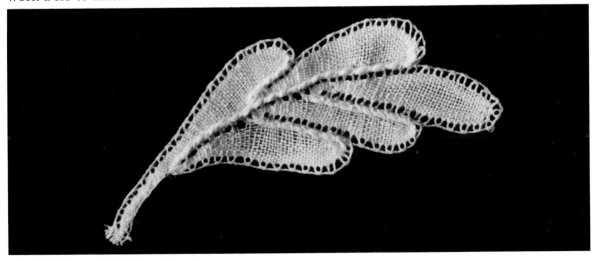

87

Leaf with double raised vein (fig. 122)

Set up at *A* with 4–2 pairs, and work a rib at *B* with pinholes on the left. Work leaf 1, and add pairs as necessary. Work the rest of the leaves in the same way as the previous ones with rolled edges.

Fig. 122. *Order of working a leaf with a double raised vein*

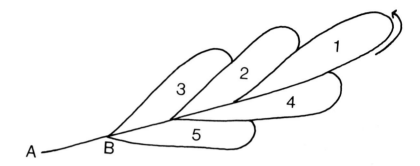

The rolled edges can also be used to finish off motifs on the outside, and to carry threads from one place to another.

The raised and rolled technique is used to a large extent in Withof Duchesse, and is extremely useful in designing and working any free lace patterns, for taking threads to other parts of the pattern, without having to finish off all the time. This makes working easier as well as tidier and it can enhance the character of the lace.

Fig. 123. *Right (front) side of a leaf with double raised vein*

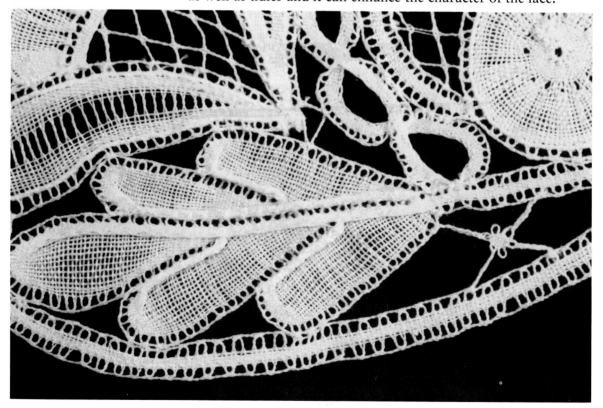

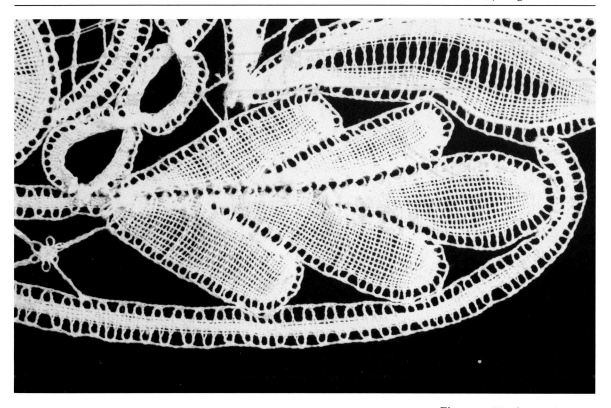

Fig. 124. *Working side of the same leaf*

Fig. 125. *a–e. Practice patterns of leaves*

Patterns

Round paperweight motif
(fig. 126; Egyptian cotton 100)

Set up the outside braid with 4–2–2 + gimp. Work this with or without picots on the outside.

Work each cloverleaf, setting up each curl with 4–2, adding gimp pair and extra pairs as you start working the leaves. Join these to the outside braid and the other cloverleaves where necessary.

Finish with the bars, picots and whole-stitch blocks. Start these on the side of the leaves by hanging in 2 pairs for the bars.

Fig. 126. *'Peter', pattern for a cloverleaf-motif*

Fig. 127. *'Peter', cloverleaf-motif*

Butterfly (fig. 128; Egyptian cotton 100–12 pairs)

Body: Start this on both sides at the top with a rib. Make sure the pinholes are on the outside. Join these ribs into a braid when you work the head. Further down decorate the body working 3 whole stitches, 3 half stitches, 3 whole stitches. Near the end work whole stitch only, and gradually lay pairs back. These can be cut off later. Finish with 2 pairs, knot these and cut them off.

Upper wings: Work the braids with 6 pairs. Fill in the edging with gimp + 9 pairs. For the hole in the wings use the method as described for berry no. 4, winding a thread round 4 or 5 support pins on the circle. Use the same-size thread as you use for the rest of

Fig. 128. *'Olive', pattern for a butterfly*

the work. The filling I used is point ground (half stitch and two twists, or cross and three twists).

Lower wings: Work a rib to outline the wings, then fill the space with tallies or whole-stitch blocks.

Fig. 129. *'Olive', butterfly*

Star of David (fig. 130; Egyptian cotton 120 with gold thread gimp)

Start the two braids simultaneously, because they overlap each other at every crossing. They are worked with 6 pairs and 2 gimp pairs.

You can work the points as corners, but if you want the turned-over corner effect, you should work each braid longer than necessary. Lengthen the lines on the pattern with a ruler for about 2cm (1in). Take the pins out until the inside corner, then turn the lace and bobbins over, put the pins back on the original pattern-line, and continue.

Work the centre flower, and fill the spaces with bars, crossing each other.

Fig. 130. *Pattern for a Star of David, very suitable for large square paperweight with light blue background*

Fig. 131. *'Star of David'*

Purse decoration (fig. 132; Egyptian cotton 100)

Work the leaf on the right first, starting at the top and finishing with
the curl. Work the other leaf, again setting up at the top. Finish off
by sewing the remaining pairs into the pinholes of the curl.

Work the berries, and connect them to the leaf stems with a braid.

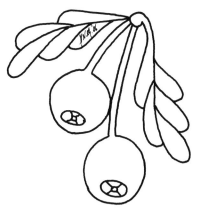

Fig. 132. *'Ella', a pattern for
a purse-motif*

Fig. 133. *'Ella', purse-motif*

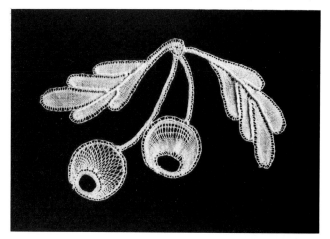

Fig. 134. *Purse and cloverleaf pendant*

Bookmark (fig. 135; Egyptian cotton 80)

Set up 4–2–2–2 + gimp for the berries. Work these as berry no. 2 (fig. 112). Work differently decorated leaves:

1. Start at a point and work 3 whole stitches on either side, with half stitches in the middle.

2. Start at a point, twist weaver 3 times in the centre.

3. Start with the stem, work one half in whole stitch, and the next half in half stitch.

4. Start at a point, work in whole or half stitch.

Fig. 135. *'Mattie',*
pattern for a bookmark

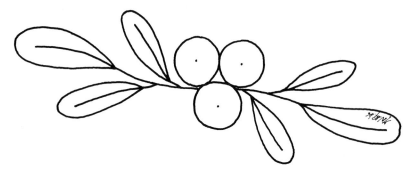

Fig. 136. *'Mattie',*
bookmark-motif

7 Three further patterns

'Remember that the most beautiful things in the world are the most useless: peacocks and lilies, for instance.'
John Ruskin[15]

In this chapter I shall give only very basic directions. If you have worked through the practice pieces, or if you already know the techniques, you will have no problems working these – or maybe I should say: not many problems.

Of course you can vary each part of a pattern according to what you like. These patterns are meant to stimulate you to use your

Fig. 137. *'Ans', handkerchief corner*

imagination, not to follow the example slavishly, unless you prefer doing just that. Remember that you can interpret a pattern your way. May I suggest that before you work it, you look at the pattern without the photograph of the finished lace. Try to visualize how you would like to see it finished.

This will also help you to design your own patterns, if you have not already done so, and to make lace that is really personal.

Handkerchief corner (fig. 138; Egyptian cotton 100)

Work the centre rib and the edge round it. Next, work the braid, and the lower rib and edge for which you can hang in pairs at the braid.

Work the inside 'leaves', and the outside edging with picots. Lastly, work the bars with picots, and the tallies.

Fig. 138. *Pattern for the handkerchief corner*

Fig. 139. *'Ans', handkerchief corner*

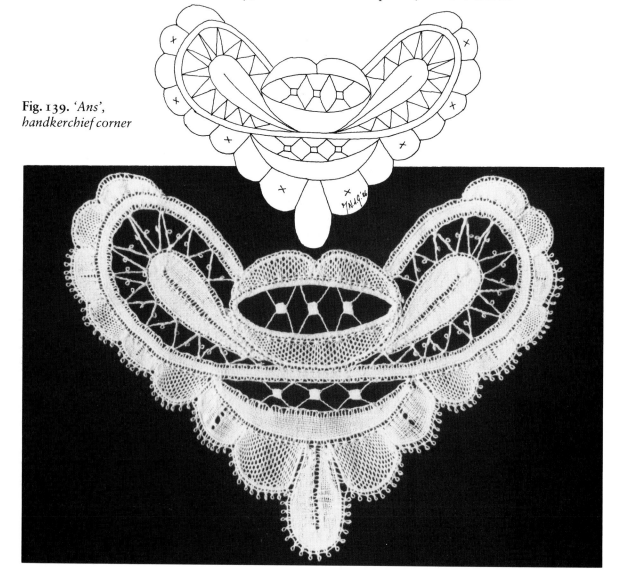

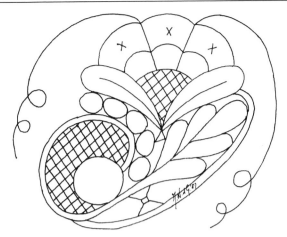

Fig. 140. *'Embryo',*
a pattern

'Embryo' (fig. 140; Egyptian cotton 100)

Start with the berry, then work the braid from the berry to work the
leaf. Change this into a rib as the leaf starts, with the pins on the
right-hand side. If you twist 3 times at the footside, it will make
sewing in easier later on. Work the two leaves underneath the
flower, setting up on the top and increasing to 14 pairs.

Set up the rib for the flower in the existing pinholes of the leaves.
The small edging is worked with 8 pairs in whole stitch. The larger
edging can still be worked with 8 pairs, if you work it in half stitch.
Work the outside braid and the 'beads'.

Finish with the fillings, the ribs coming from the flower head, and
the tally.

Fig. 141. *'Embryo'*

Finger plate (fig. 143; Egyptian cotton 100)

Start with the centre flower, which takes about 12 pairs + gimp pair. For the outside flowers start with the braid, and use the pairs from the braid to work the rib. Hang in more pairs when you work the petals. Start the large braids at the centre flower, by hanging in 4–2–2 pairs, and reduce the pairs when you connect them to the outside flower.

Work the small ribs, and hang in here the pairs for the oval shape, working towards the centre flower. Divide this shape in the middle as you work down.

The fillings are worked with whole stitch and 4 twists. Sew in one pair at each starting point.

Work the berries, and finish with the whole-stitch blocks and the tallies.

Fig. 142. *'Henny', fingerplate*

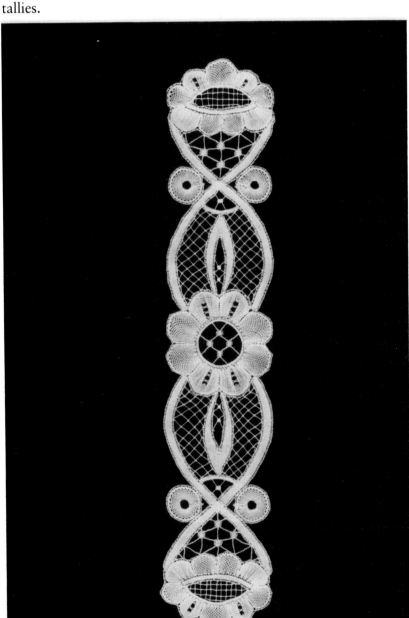

Fig. 143. 'Henny',
pattern for a fingerplate

Fig. 144. *A fish, design by*
Marijke van Wijngen

Fig. 145. *Snail,*
designed and worked by
Marijke van Wijngen

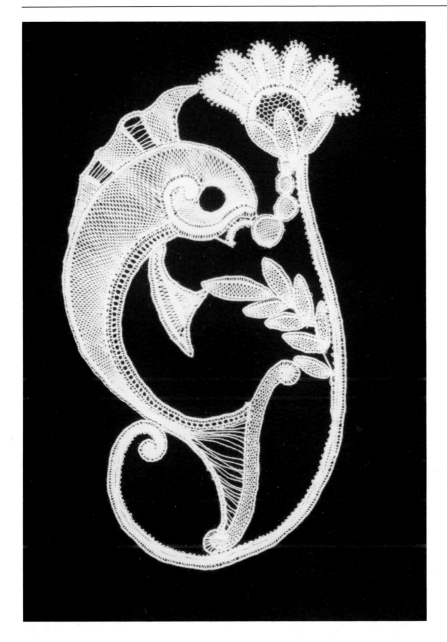

Fig. 146. *Fish, designed and worked by Marijke van Wijngen*

Fig. 147. *Pattern of snail design, by Marijke van Wijngen*

8 Mounts and frames

'Full many a flower is born to blush unseen,
and waste its sweetness on the desert air'

Thomas Gray[16]

There are many beautiful pieces of lace stored in folders and box-files that are crying out to be exhibited. Unfortunately, many lace-makers love making the lace, but hate mounting it. However, with the arrival of all kinds of different frames, the job has been made much easier. You no longer need to spend hours sewing a piece of lace on to a suitable background.

My favourite way of mounting lace pictures will always be the

Fig. 148. *Lace star hung in a glass ball*

clip-frame. Because there is no frame round it, apart from four tiny clips to keep the glass in place, the lace gets all the attention it deserves. It just hangs there, all on its own, not to be used, but waiting to be admired. Any well-designed and beautifully made piece of lace deserves this treatment, rather than being folded in tissue-paper to come out on special occasions. That said, you can only put a limited number of lace pictures on the wall, and the rest will have to be stored away, or mounted differently. I shall give a few examples and hints as to the ways and means of mounting them.

Fingerplate

Cut a piece of felt which fits snugly inside the fingerplate frame, and lay the lace on this. You can fasten it with a tiny stitch in several places or with the smallest drop of glue, but this may not be necessary. Then cut another piece of the same-colour felt, this time of the same size as the fingerplate. Lay the smaller piece with the lace on it on top of this, so that the larger piece of felt is showing on all sides. Put some suitable glue all along the edge on the back of the fingerplate, and press this on the felt. Leave it weighted down for a while, after which it will be ready to be screwed to the place where you want it.

Fig. 149. *'Henny', fingerplate-mounted*

Paperweight

Unless you want to sew the lace to the backing, this is even easier than the fingerplate, provided the rim on the paperweight is not too deep. Cut a piece of felt larger than the paperweight, or the same size, lay the lace on it, put glue along the back edge of the paperweight and put this firmly on the felt, surrounding the lace. Cut off the felt around the paperweight. For a more efficient finish, or if you want to sew it to the backing, it is better to use the same method as for the fingerplate.

Fig. 150. *'Alresford' design in paperweight*

Brooch

These often come with a piece of coloured felt already inside, but you may want a different colour or material. Use the cardboard inside the brooch to cut out the material you want, put the lace on it, and follow the instructions that usually come with these frames.

Bookmark

There are several ways of mounting these. If you use the plastic cover, put the lace on a piece of material which is the size of the bookmark-cover. I use a long paperknife to slide it inside the cover. You can use a ruler in the following way. Pull a long thread through the top of the material with the lace. Put the ruler under the material against the thread which hangs down behind the ruler. Push the material and the lace up with the ruler, holding the thread in your hand. When it is in place, remove the ruler, and carefully pull the thread away.

Handkerchief corner, insert, edging etc.

Unfortunately, there is no quick way of mounting these. You can use the three-sided stitch for Duchesse lace, or use a sewing stitch to sew through the pinholes and the material. The second method has a disadvantage in that you still have to work away the raw edge afterwards. With a three-sided stitch you can cut the material really close to the lace, but this stitch requires more patience.

When you use lace as an edging or insert, always sew it on after sewing the material together. It is really best to do this by hand.

Mounting on net

Lay the lace right side down, and place the net over it, tacking it on to the lace. You can now sew the net to the lace in the lace-pinholes. If you prefer to see what you are doing, you can put the lace on top of the net, right side up, and sew it to the net that way. I prefer not to cut the net away afterwards, as the work will hold its shape better with the net still there.

There are many more ways and methods of mounting lace. I have only given a summary, but no doubt you have come across other ideas that appeal to you.

9 Make use of your lace

'Mrs Elton, – as elegant as lace and pearls could make her . . .'

Jane Austen, *Emma*[17]

No longer do we go around wearing as much lace as we possibly can, on every occasion. Nevertheless, one look in a lingerie shop will convince anyone that lace on clothing is far from obsolete, albeit on clothes worn away from the public eye. Apart from this use of lace, there are times in fashion when lace is the rage, and you can see lace being worn in all sorts of ways, from collars and scarves to petticoats that show lace peeping out from under a skirt. Only last week I saw a girl at a supermarket check-out wearing a piece of lace-edging tied up in her hair.

Lace is timeless, and even if it is not always fashionable in clothing, you can always wear a lace-brooch or pendant – that is, if you are a 'lacy' person. There are people on whom lace would look totally wrong. Often they know this, and it does not in the least dampen their enthusiasm for making it.

So how do you use lace? I shall try to answer this question in three ways:

1. Clothes – for ladies, men and children
2. Domestic use
3. Gifts

Clothes for ladies

If you don't like wearing lace, and feel it is too pretty and feminine, have you ever thought of making a large brooch with an abstract design? Lace does not have to be 'pretty' to be effective. However, for those who like to wear lace in whatever shape or form, there are endless ways in which to use it in your clothing. For example, have you thought of using a special motif appliquéd to a corner of your favourite scarf? You could put several different-size flowers together in a cunning way, and end up with a rather unusual brooch, or, if you do this on a larger scale, a jabot for that very special dress.

Fig. 151. *'Dilys', insert for blouse*

Handkerchiefs do not only have lace edges and corners, they look quite different with a lace flower insert. Pockets on blouses can look rather dull, until you put a decorative motif on them. A beautiful blouse looks even better with a lace insert in its sleeves (fig. 151). If you like embroidering you can combine that with lace, and look very original.

Then, of course, there is the collar. Not only the attractive wide flouncy collar, but also a simple edge on a collar can make all the difference to a plain dress.

A very traditional and much appreciated way to use lace is on a wedding-veil, and anyone who has done this knows that it is well worth the effort.

Clothes for men

Not all men like the idea of wearing lace. There is, however, nothing unmanly about wearing lace. History is full of men with lace collars and edgings on their clothes. Even in our modern time lace is worn by men in some form. I have seen ties appliquéd with coloured lace, very stylish and original.

There are still shirts for sale with lace edgings, so why not have a handmade lace edging? Duchesse and Honiton lace lend themselves very well to making tiny motifs of favourite hobbies to put on ties or shirts.

Remember, the only limit is your imagination!

Clothes for children

For many children, the first occasion on which they wear lace is their christening. Anyone who went to see the OIDFA exhibition in Brighton in the summer of 1986 will still remember the beautiful christening gown exhibited on the Dutch stall. It was Withof Duchesse lace, and made with imagination and endless patience.

Usually, children like lace (fig. 152). It is possible to use coloured thread and make motifs to put on blouses, dresses, even mittens. But it is also possible to do the same with white or cream thread. Maybe you remember, not very long ago, that it was fashionable to put lace edgings around girls' socks. Could it have been a lace-maker who first thought of the idea?

Fig. 152. *Author's daughter wearing lace-motif*

Domestic use

From ancient times women have thought of ways to decorate everyday domestic things. When you study history, you will find lots of references to needle-work and embroidery. Even at the time of the Exodus of the Jews out of Egypt, generally accepted to have been around 1500 BC, there are references to a doorhanging 'the work of a needleworker, or embroiderer' (Exodus 36:37 Authorized Version). Later, there is a reference to 'women who weave net-works' (Isaiah 19:9).

We know that in many Eastern countries there are beautiful tapestries, and embroidered domestic items, which make our modern homes look rather colourless. But there are many ways in which we too can transform 'ordinary' things into items that are a pleasure to use.

A friend of mine renovated a guest-towel by putting a lace strip over one end, and with this added yet another beautiful thing to her home. Napkins in rings decorated with a lace strip or motif make a dinner-table look quite festive. And how do you feel opening a door which has a fingerplate with a delightful lace-design in it? You don't have to be a 'lacy' person to appreciate this sort of beauty.

Fig. 153. *Corner, designed by Nora Ummels*

Lace in the home can be much more than lace mats and wall-decorations. Motifs or inserts can be used for a tea-cosy, a cushion, a cheerful tablecloth for the garden furniture, with matching seat-covers or cushions. A tray can be made attractive by a lace-edged cloth, and a lampshade looks totally different with a lace insertion or motif.

In Holland it is customary to have window-decorations as well as wall-hangings. Round and square-shaped thin metal frames are used for this. Make sure that the lace is held tightly inside it and does not sag. You can do this by leaving the lace on the pillow, putting the frame round it and then fastening the lace to the frame. Ideally, the lace should be about 2cm (1in) smaller than the frame. If you

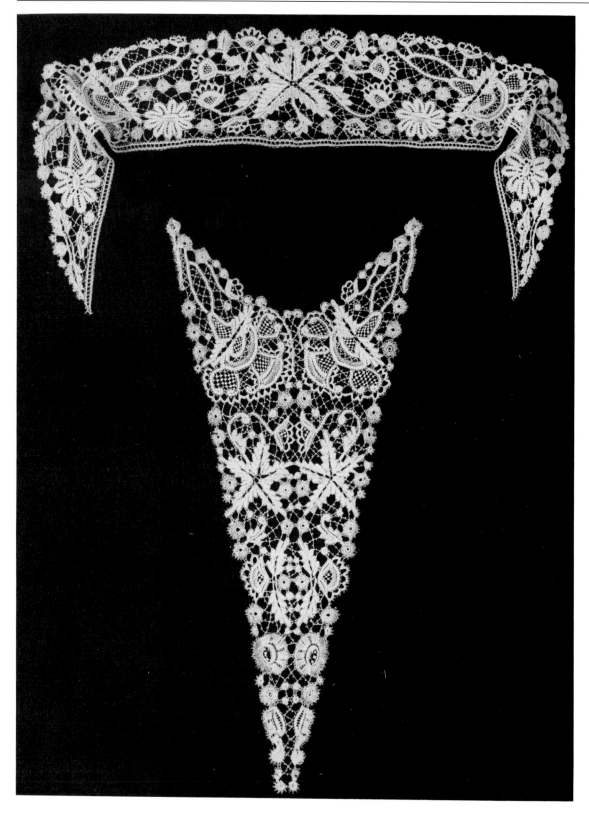

oversew the frame beforehand with a buttonhole stitch (the least attractive part of the job!) you will find it easier to attach the lace to the frame at strategic points – not too far apart.

Gifts

Finding a suitable gift for someone can be a real problem sometimes. For those of us who make lace it can become a real pleasure. There are many craft shops and suppliers of lacemaking materials who sell countless frames and mounts in all shapes and sizes, from little folding ash-trays to heavy paperweights, most of them even gift-boxed!

The wonderful thing about paperweights is that they can be given to male friends. Do try to find a suitable design. Most men like strong, bold designs, and these can also be worked in delicate lace types.

For ladies, the choice appears to be endless. Pretty handkerchiefs, lavender bags trimmed with ribbon and lace edges, brooches, pendants, little 'pots for putting things in', pill-boxes, and of course the many dressing-table items that can be decorated with lace. Not all women like these things, however, and it can be a challenge to think of something suitable and original.

I am sure that, as you try to use the lace you make, you will discover many new ideas for displaying your lace in some way. You can provide a very personal touch by sending a Christmas card with a lace motif on. The first card to arrive this year was one of those, sent by a special friend.

Do make sure that you give lace to someone who appreciates it for what it is. Especially if you have taken a long time over making something special, it deserves to be presented in the best possible way, so that you get the praise you deserve.

Fig. 154. *A collar and jabot, worked in Sluis, by Martha Berkers, ca 1910–35*
Real size of collar is 43/9cm (17/3½in)
Real size of jabot is 28/13cm (11/5in)
Reproduced by permission of Rijksmuseum, Amsterdam

10 Designing your own lace patterns

'To find new motifs for her lace-designs, in the winter Julie poured some water on a sheet of glass, and watched to see how ice-crystals were formed as the water touched the glass. Then she traced these arabesques onto transparent paper . . . They had seen many of these feather-light pieces of lace in the house.'

Henry Troyat[18]

One of the greatest joys of lacemaking is to work a piece of lace that you have designed yourself. It is also an excellent way to learn. Instead of carefully following instructions in a book, you now have to solve problems on your own.

When you have finished a piece of lace, you have created something original and unique. To design your own patterns, you do not have to be especially gifted or clever, as long as you have some imagination. However, you do need a thorough knowledge of the technique, to be able to use it to full advantage. Only when you know the reason for certain rules in lace-making can you use them, and, if necessary, break them.

When you have learnt the techniques of Duchesse lace, it is relatively easy to design in this lace-type, as you can vary the number of bobbins during the work. Of course, it is important to retain the character of the Duchesse technique, if you want to call your lace Duchesse. Opinions differ as to what can be included, and what should be left out. Mrs v.d. Meulen-Nulle, who was without doubt a leading, if not *the* leading figure in Duchesse design, had no hesitation in using the leaf-shaped tallies as a filling, whereas many modern Duchesse workers seem to feel that these should be left out. With the arrival of Zr. Judith's 'Withof- Duchesse' a new dimension to Duchesse lace was created, but the basic character of Duchesse has been beautifully preserved.

All this shows that lace-making is not a 'dead' art, and that there is a lot of scope for invention and creativity. Apart from this, you can of course use the Duchesse techniques very effectively in modern 'free lace' design.

There are a few important points to remember when you start designing. As design in Latin means 'planning', it is necessary to think over some points before you start making the lace you have designed, or even before you start drawing the design.

Fig. 155. *Development of the finger plate design*

Composition

Just as with photography and painting, a basic rule is that there should not be any strong lines leading the eye away out of the picture. The whole piece has to be pleasing and give a sense of completeness, unless you want a deliberately disturbing design. Use areas of whole stitch and braids and fillings in a creative, balanced way to get an attractive result.

Purpose

In designing you should keep in mind the purpose for which the lace is going to be used. Think of the final effect of the lace, when you start a design for something special. Very often the shape or size of the mount will inspire the design for it. The idea of Duchesse for a fingerplate made me think of an hour-glass, and it was that which inspired the fingerplate design (fig 155).

At other times a piece of lace that you have finished will itself help you to decide how to mount it. Looking at the finished 'embryo' design, I decided that it would have to go in an oval frame.

Drawing the pattern

Make sure that a symmetrical design really is symmetrical. You can do this by using graph-paper and a ruler or compass. Indicate on the pattern-drawing how you want to work it. Try to plan the best way of starting and finishing off, so that the result will be as tidy as possible.

Finally, when you draw an asymmetrical design which looks pleasing, turn it over, so that when you finally have finished, and turn it the right way round again, you will get the picture that you liked so much in the first place, and not a mirror-image. I know from experience that it is easy to forget this.

Sources of inspiration

Personally I like to study flowers and other things in nature, to see how I can best reflect the true character of something, when I have to work it in a stylized way. Stamps and postcards also give me many ideas for designs. I keep the postcards, calender pictures etc. that I find attractive, and look through them from time to time. Illustrations in books and encyclopedias can be very inspiring too. One of the ingredients for successful designing is to become observant, and use your imagination. The more you design, the more you get used to 'translating' what you see into lace.

Most important of all, keep a note of anything that occurs to you,

Fig. 156. *'Delwyn', pattern based on wood-carving in the pulpit of St John's Church, Alresford, Hampshire*

by simple little sketches for example, and put them all together in a file. Then, when you are stuck for ideas, leaf through the papers in the file, and you will find that inspiration comes back.

Tools you may need

White/graph/tracing paper
Pencils, fineline drawing pens, rubber
Ruler, set of mathematical instruments
Plastic sheets with ovals, circles and other shapes cut out. These are extremely useful.

Remember, your basic tool is your imagination, and you can develop that. It is possible to base a lace design on something you read, as the poem and picture illustrate.

Ode to Alresford

A child in Holland – dreaming of the hills
in which ploughed fields rise up to meet
proud woods parading on the ridge,
stooping and rising with defiant ease;

an ancient farmhouse hidden in the shade
of comforting, protective trees;

a sandy lane losing its way, secluded
among hedgerows through the fields;

a friendly unexpected town, surrounded by
green hills and clear fresh water springs;
a church with bells; a station in the age of steam;
Alresford in Hampshire – fulfilment of my dream.

Fig. 157. *'Alresford', a pattern*

Finally, when you look at other people's work, comparing it with your own, don't be put off if you feel that it is better than yours. Keep practising, and one day you will look back on things you made earlier, knowing where you could do better now.

Fig. 158. *'Alresford'*

All the time – think positively. Cultivate healthy self-criticism, which means seeing the good as well as the bad. Try to improve your work constantly, and think of new things to make. Learn from your mistakes, don't let them discourage you.

I do hope this book has helped you to enjoy making Duchesse lace as much as I enjoy it, and I look forward to seeing many new Duchesse designs.

A step-by-step symmetrical design

(*a*) Initial sketch of a pulpit wood-engraving in St John's Church, Alresford, done in a hurry, while house-hunting in Hampshire.

(*b*) Draw basic shapes (squares, circles and diagonal lines, easiest done on graph-paper) to provide the groundwork for easier drawing later on. Draw outlines of the main parts, and decide on the shape of the centre flower.

(*c*) Finish outlines and experiment with the shape and position of the small flowers. Because of the position of the petals, flower A accentuates the pointed ends of the design, and flower B makes the design look shorter and more square.

(*d*) Decide which filling to use, and experiment with other details, e.g. braid, edge, flower-petals.

Fig. 159. *a–d. A step-by-step design*

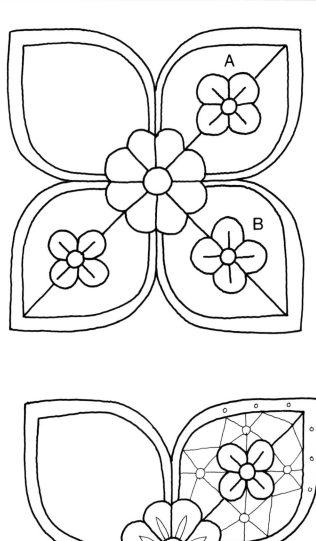

References

1 LOUISA TEBBS, *The art of bobbin lace*, Chapman and Hall, 1907, p. 89. Reprinted in 1978 by Paul Minet.

2 RICHARD JEFFERIES, *The old house at Coates*, Lutterworth Press, 1948, p. 190.

3 D. W. WOERTMAN/J. HERBERT, *Mutsen en streekdrachten in Gelderland en Overijssel, Historie*, 1977, p. 131.

4 RAINER MARIA RILKE, *The notebook of Malte Laurids Brigge*, Oxford University Press, 1984, p. 131.

5 G. HEUVELMAN, 'De Nederlandsche Kantwerkschool', in *Eigen Haard*, 1902, p. 805.

6 ibid., p. 828.

7 L.W.v.d.MEULEN-NULLE, *Handleiding tot het vervaardigen van Duchesse kant*, The Hague, 1907, Terra Zutphen, reprinted in 1923, and 1983.

8 M. MACKINTOSH, 'Kanttekeningen bij een kantkenster', in *Bij Voorbeeld*, 1969, pp. 56–9.

9 L.W.v.d.MEULEN-NULLE, *Kant met naald en klos en speldenbos*, Bussum, 1959.

10 WILLIAM COWPER, *Table-talk*, John Sharpe, London, 1825.

11 A. T. QUILLER-COUCH, *Ship of stars*, 1899, ch. 13.

12 ALEXANDER POPE, *An essay on criticism*, 1711, 2.45.

13 WALTER DE LA MARE, *The collected poems of Walter de la Mare*, Faber and Faber, 1979, p. 111.

14 JOHN CLARE, in ROBIN HOLMES, *A country calendar of rural rhymes*, Eyre Methuen, 1980 p. 25.

15 JOHN RUSKIN, *The stones of Venice*, 1851–53, Vol. I, 2.17.

16 THOMAS GRAY, *Elegy written in a Country Churchyard*, 1742–50.

17 JANE AUSTEN, *Emma*, 1816, ch. 34.

18 HENRI TROYAT, 'Jeugdige harstochten', pp. 16–7. trs. Johan Frederik, Bigot & van Rossum, 1970. Translation into English by author of *Duchesse Lace*.

Bibliography

ANNELIE VAN OLFFEN, *De techniek van het kantklossen*, Cantecleer, 1979

L.W.v.d.MEULEN-NULLE, *Handleiding tot het vervaardigen van Duchessekant*, Terra Zutphen, 1983

L.W.v.d.MEULEN-NULLE, *Lace*, London, 1963

ZUS BOELAARS, *Kantlossen slag voor slag*, Cantecleer, 1977

CARMEN ACKET-de MEZA, *Kloskant*

JOSE van PAMELEN-HAGENAARS, *Duchesse*, Pieters b.v.

NEL LEEUWRIK, *Kantklosplezier*, Terra Zutphen

LOUISA TEBBS, *The art of bobbin-lace*, Chapman and Hall, 1907

BRIGITTE BELLON, *Klöppeln*, Frech-Verlag, Stuttgart, 1980.

ANN COLLIER, *Creative design in bobbin-lace*, Batsford, 1982

ANN COLLIER, *The art of lacemaking*, David & Charles, 1986

Duchesse, *Dentelle à fils rapportés*, Lace Centre, Le Puy.

PAVOL MICHALIDES, *Dentelles de notre temps*, Elena Holeczyova, Paris, 1978

EMILY REIGATE, *An illustrated guide to lace*, Antique Collectors Club, 1986

SANTINA LEVEY, *Lace, a history*, Maney, 1983

I. YEFINOVA, *Russian embroidery and lace*, Hudson and Taylor, 1987

Embroidery:

ALBARTA MEULENBELT-NIEUWBURG, *Embroidery motifs from Dutch samplers*, Batsford, 1974

JANE ILES, *Old English roses in needlework*, David & Charles

EMMY VAN VRIJBERGER-de CONINGH, *Streekdrachtmotieven*, Becht, Amsterdam, 1983

Collections of lace

Holland:

Rijksmuseum – Amsterdam
Museum Boymans van Beuningen – Rotterdam
Openlucht museum – Arnhem
Centraal museum – Utrecht
Oudheidkamer – Ommen (Tel. 05291–6811 or 3487)

Belgium:

Gruuthuuse museum – Bruges
Kantcentrum – Bruges
Musées Royaux d'Art et d'Histoire – Brussels

France:

Lace museum and school – Le Puy
Lace museum – Bayeux

Britain:

Victoria and Albert Museum – London
Lace museum – Honiton
Art gallery and museum – Luton

Suppliers

United Kingdom
Alby Lace Museum
Cromer Road
Alby
Norfolk
NR11 7QE

Bedford Lace
4 Newnham Street
Bedford

Ann Brock
1 Ingham Close
Blake Hall Road
Mirfield
Yorkshire

Campden Needlecraft Centre
High Street
Chipping Campden
Gloucestershire

Chosen Crafts Centre
46 Winchcombe Street
Cheltenham
Gloucestershire
GL52 2ND

Margaret Clark
Mount Vernon
Lyme Road
Higher Poynton
Stockport
Cheshire
SK12 1TH

Leonie Cox
The Old School
Childswickham
Near Broadway
Worcs
WR12 7HD

J. and J. Ford
October Hill
Upper Way
Upper Longdon
Rugeley
Staffordshire
WS15 1QB

Framecraft
83 Hampstead Road
Handsworth Wood
Birmingham
B2L 1JA

Mr R. Gravestock
Highwood
Crews Hill
Alfrick
Worcestershire
WR6 5HF

Hepatica
82a Water Lane
Wilmslow
Cheshire

Frank Herring & Sons
27 High West Street
Dorshester
Dorset
DT1 1UP

Honiton Lace Shop
44 High Street
Honiton
Devon

D. J. Hornsby
149 High Street
Burton Latimer
Kettering
Northants
NN15 5RL
and
25 Manwood Avenue
Canterbury
Kent
CT2 7AH

Needlestyle
24–6 West Street
Alresford
Hampshire

Jane's Pincushion
Wroxham Barns
Tunstead Road
Hoveton
Norwich
NR12 2QU

All branches of John Lewis

Lambourn Valley Cottage
Industries
11 Oxford Street
Lambourn
Berks
RG16 7XS

Mace and Nairn
89 Crane Street
Salisbury
Wiltshire
SP1 2PY

Iris Martin
Farthing Cottage
Clickers Yard
Yardley Road
Olney
Bucks

Needle Work
Ann Bartlet
Bucklers Farm
Coggeshall
Essex
CO6 1SB

The Needlewoman
21 Needless Abbey
off New Street
Birmingham
B2 5AE

T. Parker
124 Corhampton Road
Boscombe East
Bournemouth
BH6 5NZ

Dorothy Pearce
5 Fulshaw Avenue
Wilmslow
Cheshire
SK9 5IA

Jane Playford
North Lodge
Church Close
West Runton
Norfolk
NR27 9QY

Christine Riley
53 Barclay Street
Stonehaven
Kincardineshire
Scotland

Pat Savory
Tanglewood
4 Sanden Close
Hungerford
Berks
RGI7 0LB

Peter and Beverley Scarlett
Strupak
Hill Head
Coldwells
Ellon
Grampian

Ken and Pat Schultz
134 Wisbech Road
Thornley
Peterborough

J. S. Sear
Lacecraft Supplies
8 Hill View
Sherrington
Buckinghamshire

Sebalace
Waterloo Mills
Howden Road
Silsden
W. Yorks
BD2 0HA

A. Sells
49 Pedley Lane
Clifton
Shefford
Bedfordshire

Shireburn Lace
Finkle Court
Finkle Hill
Sherburn in Elmet
N. Yorks
LS25 6EB

Stephen Simpson
Avenham Road Works
Preston
Lancs

Stitches
Dovehouse Shopping Parade
Warwick Road
Olton
Solihull
West Midlands

S.M.P.
4 Garners Close
Chalfont St Peter
Bucks
SL9 0HB

Teazle Embroideries
35 Boothferry Road
Hull
North Humberside

Valley House Crafts Studios
Ruston
Scarborough
N. Yorks

George Walker
The Corner Shop
Rickinghall
Diss
Norfolk

George White
Delaheys Cottage
Thistle Hill
Knareborough
N. Yorks
HG5 8LS

Bobbins
A. R. Archer
The Poplars
Shelland
Near Stowmarket
Suffolk
IPI4 3DE

T. Brown
Temple Lane Cottage
Littledean
Cinderford
Gloucestershire

Bridge Bookshop
7 Bridge Street
Bath
Avon
B82 4AS

Stephen Cook
'Cottage Crafts'
6 Woodlands Close
Flackwell Heath
Buckinghamshire
HP10 9EP

Chrisken Bobbins
26 Cedar Drive
Kingsclere
Newbury
Bucks
RGI5 8TD

Malcolm J. Fielding
2 Northern Terrace
Moss Lane
Silverdale
Lancs
LA5 0ST

Richard Gravestock
Highwood
Crews Hill
Alfrick
Worcestershire
WR6 5HF

Larkfield Crafts
Hilary Rickitts
4 Island Cottages
Mapledurwall
Basingstoke
Hants
RG25 2LU

Lambourn Valley Cottage
Industries
II Oxford Street
Lambourn
Berks
RGI6 7XS

T. Parker
124 Corhampton Road
Boscombe East
Bournemouth
BH6 5NZ

Bryn Phillips
'Pantglas'
Cellan
Dyfed
Lampeter
SA48 8JD

D. H. Shaw
47 Zamor Crescent
Thruscroft
Rotherham
S. Yorks
S66 9QD

Sizelands
1 Highfield Road
Winslow
Bucks
MK10 3QU

Christine and David Springett
21 Hillmorton Road
Rugby
Warwickshire
CV22 5DF

Richard Viney
Unit 7
Port Royal Street
Southsea
Hants
PO5 4NP

George White
Delaheys Cottage
Thistle Hill
Knaresborough
N. Yorks

Lace pillows
Newnham Lace Equipment
15 Marlowe Close
Basingstoke
Hants
RG24 9DD

Books
Bridge Bookshop
7 Bridge Street
Bath
Avon
BS2 4AS

Craft Bookcase
29 London Road
Sawbridgeworth
Herts
CM21 9EH

Christopher Williams
19 Morrison Avenue
Parkstone
Poole
Dorset
BH12 4AD

Silk embroidery and lace thread
E. and J. Piper
Silverlea
Flax Lane
Glemsford
Suffolk
CO10 7RS

Silk weaving yarn
Hilary Chetwynd
Kipping Cottage
Cheriton
Alresford
Hants
SO24 0PW

Frames and mounts
Doreen Campbell
'Highcliff'
Bremilham Road
Malmesbury
Wilts

Matt coloured transparent adhesive film
Heffers Graphic Shop
26 King Street
Cambridge
CB1 1LN

United States of America
Arbor House
22 Arbor Lane
Roslyn Hights
NY 11577

Baltazor Inc
3262 Severn Avenue
Metairie
LA 7002

Beggars' Lace
P.O. Box 17263
Denver
Colorado 80217

Berga Ullman Inc.
P.O. Box 918
North Adams
Massachusetts 01247

Frederick J. Fawcett
129 South Street
Boston
Massachusetts 02130

Frivolité
15526 Densmore N.
Seattle
Washington 98113

Happy Hands
3007 S. W. Marshall
Pendleton
Oregon 97180

International Old Lacers
P.O. Box 1029
Westminster
Colorado 80030

Lace Place de Belgique
800 S.W. 17th Street
Boca Raton
FL 33432

Lacis
2150 Stuart Street
Berkeley
California 9470

Robin's Bobbins
RTL Box 1736
Mineral Bluff
Georgia 30559

Robin and Russ Handweavers
533 North Adams Street
McMinnvills
Oregon 97128

Some Place
2990 Adline Street
Berkeley
California 94703

Osma G. Todd Studio
319 Mendoza Avenue
Coral Gables
Florida 33134

The Unique And Art Lace Cleaners
5926 Delman Boulevard
St Louis
Missouri 63112

Van Scriver Bobbin Lace
130 Cascadilla Park
Ithaca
New York 14850

The World in Stiches
82 South Street
Milford
N.H. 03055

Australia
Dentelles Lace Supplies
3 Narrak Close
Jindalee
Queensland 4074

The Lacemaker
94 Fordham Avenue
Hartwell
Victoria 3124

Spindle and Loom
Arcade 83
Longueville Road
Lane Cove
NSW 2066

Tulis Crafts
201 Avoca Street
Randwick
NSW 2031

Belgium
't Handwerkhuisje
Katelijnestraat 23
8000 Bruges
Belgium

Kantcentrum
Balstraat 14
8000 Bruges

Manufacture Belge de Dentelle
6 Galerie de la Reine
Galeries Royales St Hubert
1000 Bruxelles

Orchidee
Mariastraat 18
8000 Bruges

France
Centre d'Initiation a la Dentelle du
Puy
2 Rue Duguesclin
43000 Le Puy en Velay

A L'Econome
Anne-Marie Deydier
Ecole de Dentelle aux Fuseaux
10 rue Paul Chenavard
69001 Lyon

Rougier and Ple
13–15 bd des Filles de Calvaire
75003 Paris

West Germany
Der Fenster Laden
Berliner Str 8
D 6483 Bad Soden
Salmunster

P. P. Hempel
Ortolangweg 34
1000 Berlin 47

Heikona De Ruijter
Kloeppelgrosshandel
Langer Steinweg 38
D4933 Blomberg

Holland
Blokker's Boektiek
Bronteeweg 4/4a
2101 AC Heemstede

Theo Brejaart
Postbus 5199
3008 AD Rotterdam

Magazinijn *De Vlijt*
Lijnmarkt 48
Utrecht

Switzerland
Fadehax
Inh. Irene Solca
4105 Biel-Benken
Basel

New Zealand
Peter McLeavey
P.O. Box 69.007
Auckland 8

Sources of information

The Lace Guild
The Hollies
53 Audnam
Stourbridge
West Midlands
DY8 4AE

The Lace Society
Linwood
Stratford Road
Oversley
Alcester
Warwickshire
BY9 6PG

The British College of Lace
21 Hillmorton Road
Rugby
Warwickshire
CV22 5DF

The English Lace School
Honiton Court
Rockbeare
Nr Exeter
Devon

International Old Lacers
President
Gunvor Jorgensen
366 Bradley Avenue
Northvale
NJ 076647
United States

United Kingdom Director of
International Old Lacers
S. Hurst
4 Dollis Road
London
N3 1RG

Ring of Tatters
Mrs C. Appleton
Nonesuch
5 Ryeland Road
Ellerby
Saltburn by Sea
Cleveland
TS13 5LP

Index

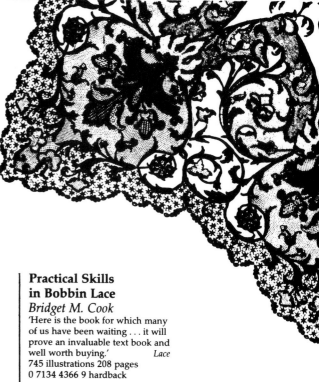